SHAKESPEARE MADE EASY

MODERN ENGLISH VERSION
SIDE-BY-SIDE WITH FULL ORIGINAL TEXT

The Taming of the Shrew

EDITED AND RENDERED INTO MODERN ENGLISH BY

Gayle Holste

All inquiries should be addressed to:
Barron's Educational Series, Inc.
250 Wireless Boulevard
Hauppauge, NY 11788
www.barronseduc.com

ISBN-13: 978-0-7641-4190-4
ISBN-10: 0-7641-4190-2

Library of Congress Catalog Card No. 2008026001

Library of Congress Cataloging-in-Publication Data

Shakespeare, William, 1564–1616.
The taming of the shrew / edited and rendered into modern English by Gayle Holste.
   p.   cm.—(Shakespeare made easy)
Includes bibiliographical references.
ISBN-13: 978-0-7641-4190-4
ISBN-10: 0-7641-4190-2
1. Man-woman relationships—Drama.   2. Married people—Drama.
3. Padua (Italy)—Drama.   4. Sex role—Drama.   I. Holste, Gayle.
II. Title.

PR2832.A25   2008
822.3'3—dc22   2008026001

PRINTED IN THE UNITED STATES OF AMERICA

9 8 7 6 5 4

Contents

Introduction

Shakespeare Made Easy is designed to help those who struggle with Shakespeare's language read his plays with greater ease and comprehension. William Shakespeare wrote his plays to appeal to a wide audience, but in the approximately four hundred years since the plays were written, the English language has undergone significant changes. Consequently, although Shakespeare is regarded by many as the greatest playwright in the English language, readers often find the language barrier insurmountable. Even though it is possible, with practice, to read the plays in the original language, many find the task too difficult and give up either in disgust or despair. Footnotes are helpful, but they can interrupt the flow of the language, and many readers become so discouraged with having to refer to footnotes that they simply give up.

Shakespeare Made Easy offers a helping hand not only to those who want to get better acquainted with Shakespeare's plays for their own sake but also to those who are required to study the plays but find the task of deciphering the language overwhelming. Of course, there is no substitute for reading and studying the plays themselves in Shakespeare's own words. The unmatched beauty of the language can never be duplicated, but the modern version will assist the reader in distinguishing between the characters and in understanding what is happening in the play.

There are a number of possible ways to use *Shakespeare Made Easy*. One option is to read the play in the original language, referring to the modern version only when necessary. Another possibility is to read the entire play in the modern version to know what is going on and then to read the original with this knowledge firmly in mind. The bracketed notations concerning the ways in which lines may be spoken by an actor—although giving only one of the possible interpretations—can be especially helpful. If the reader plans to view a filmed version of the play, reading the modern version in advance can help overcome the difficulty of trying to understand the spoken language, as well.

Whichever method you use, *Shakespeare Made Easy* will prove a valuable resource for your study of the play. It is not intended as a substitute for the original play, since even the most careful "translation" of the text will lose certain aspects such as poetic meter, alliteration, and verbal humor.

Whether you are studying the play for a class or reading it for enjoyment or to increase your acquaintance with Shakespeare's works, the Activities section at the end of the book will be helpful in pointing out themes or issues that may have escaped your notice as you read. If you need to write a paper about this play, this section will help you generate topic ideas. It will also help you as you write the paper to make sure that you have correctly interpreted a quote you are using in support of one of your points.

Using *Shakespeare Made Easy* will pave your way to a far better understanding of and appreciation for Shakespeare's plays and will remove the textual difficulties that may have caused you to stumble in past attempts. Not only will you gain confidence in discussing the plot and characters of the play, but you will also develop a greater awareness of the ways in which Shakespeare used language for poetic expression as well as for raising intriguing and challenging moral and philosophical issues.

Ever since the works of William Shakespeare entered the canon of English literature, they have excited the admiration of generations of scholars, readers, and theatergoers. Even if you've had negative experiences in the past with Shakespeare's plays—in fact, especially if you've had negative experiences— you will find yourself pleasantly surprised at just how entertaining his plays can be. We're glad you've chosen *Shakespeare Made Easy* as a companion on your journey to a better understanding of the plays of William Shakespeare.

William Shakespeare

His Life

Considering the impact that William Shakespeare has had on English literature, surprisingly little is known about his life. We do know that he was born to a prominent wool and leather merchant and his wife in 1564 (the actual day is in doubt but tradition sets it at April 23) in Stratford-upon-Avon, England. He is believed to have been educated at the local grammar school, although no lists of pupils survive from the sixteenth century. He did not attend university.

We also know from parish records that he married Anne Hathaway in 1582 when he was eighteen and she was twenty-six. They had three children; Susanna was their eldest, followed by twins, Judith and Hamnet. Their son, Hamnet, died at the age of about eleven, but the two daughters, Susanna and Judith, reached adulthood.

There are many stories about Shakespeare's life, such as the one alleging that he fled Stratford after having been caught poaching deer in the park belonging to Sir Thomas Lucy, a local justice of the peace. Like the rest of the tales about Shakespeare during this period of his life, this story cannot be verified and is probably untrue. Because his plays demonstrate extensive knowledge about a variety of subjects, articles have been written "proving" that Shakespeare must have temporarily pursued a career in either law, botany, or medicine or spent time as a soldier or sailor, to name a few of the occupations that he is speculated to have had.

The truth is, we simply don't know for sure what Shakespeare did for a living in the ten years following his marriage to Anne Hathaway. Ordinarily, as the eldest son he would have been expected to take over his father's business, but again there is no evidence to show that he did (or, for that matter, did not) serve an apprenticeship to his father. He may have spent some time with a traveling troupe of actors, but, aside from the baptismal records for his children, we have no actual records about him from the time of his marriage to Hathaway until 1592, by which time he had left Stratford and traveled to London. His wife and children remained in Stratford.

The next documented evidence pertaining to Shakespeare comes in 1592, when Shakespeare received his first critical recognition. It came in the form of a petulant outburst by fellow playwright Robert Greene who, apparently annoyed by the attention being received by this newcomer, complained bitterly in a pamphlet written from his deathbed about the "upstart crow . . . Shake-scene."

From about 1594 onward, Shakespeare was associated with a new theatrical company, The Lord Chamberlain's Men; by 1599 Shakespeare had become a shareholder in the company. The troupe gave command performances for Queen Elizabeth I as well as her successor, King James I. After King James' accession to the throne, the troupe took the name "The King's Men."

The King's Men performed at *The Globe* theater, which they owned. Of course, *The Globe* was not the only theater in London. *The Curtain* (built in 1577) and *The Rose* (1587), as well as a number of other theaters, also provided entertainment to the citizens. In addition to these open-air "public" theaters, there were many "private" or indoor theaters. Shakespeare and his friends purchased one of the private theaters, *The Blackfriars*, which was giving them especially stiff competition because of the popularity of the child actors who performed there.

With so many theaters in operation, the demand for plays was high. Shakespeare may have earned a living for a time by reworking older plays and by collaborating with others on new ones, and of course he also wrote his own plays. In addition to the uncertainty about many facts pertaining to his life, there even is debate about the exact number of plays Shakespeare wrote; some say he wrote thirty-seven, others say thirty-eight.

Shakespeare stopped writing for the stage in about 1611, and, having prospered not only from his writing but also from his shares in the theatrical company, he retired to Stratford, where he installed his family in New Place, one of the more expensive homes in Stratford. He died at the age of fifty-two on April 23, 1616.

His Plays

Many people are surprised to learn that none of the original handwritten manuscripts of Shakespeare's plays survives. At that time, plays were not considered to be "literature" in the same way that poetry was. In fact, when Shakespeare wrote his plays, they would have been the property of the producing company, which was concerned, not with publication of the plays, but with producing them on stage. The company would have bought them for about ten pounds apiece, and when a play finished its theatrical run and the copies were of no further use to the company, they often were discarded.

Roughly half of Shakespeare's plays were published during his lifetime in quarto (17 centimeters by 21 centimeters) volumes, although many of these were pirated copies. Booksellers often would hire someone to take shorthand notes during a performance, and then they would sell these unauthorized copies. This method for acquiring a copy of the play, needless to say, could result in numerous errors depending on the accuracy of the transcriber. In other instances of piracy, actors' scripts were purchased by a bookseller after the play had completed its run, but since each actor's copy would contain only his scenes, the actor would have to provide the rest of the text from memory, which often proved faulty. These pirated copies are referred to as "bad" Quartos. Even when a printer was working from a good manuscript (probably a prompt copy obtained from the theater), mistakes often contaminated the printed copy. In addition to all these problems, portions of the plays were sometimes censored for a variety of reasons, resulting in still further corruption of the text.

Fortunately, seven years after Shakespeare's death an authoritative version of his works, the First Folio (21 centimeters by 34 centimeters), edited by two of his theatrical partners and fellow actors, John Hemming and Henry Condell, was published. They claimed in the introduction to have used his original manuscripts, but that claim is unverified. The First Folio contained thirty-six of his plays and was titled *Comedies, Histories, and Tragedies*. Despite the Folio's apparent superiority to other printings of Shakespeare's plays, serious questions remain, and debate continues concerning discrepancies between the various early editions.

Because of the discrepancies between different editions of the plays, when one of Shakespeare's plays is published, editors must make decisions about which version to use. Often, the edition will contain lines from several of the oldest texts, but since in some cases there remains significant disagreement about which text is the "best" or most accurate, the reader may discover that there are differences between editions of the play. Many editions include notes at the end of the play to indicate the words or lines that have an alternate reading.

His Theater

In Elizabethan times, the London authorities viewed playgoing as both morally and politically questionable; they also believed that the large crowds that attended the plays created an increased risk for spreading the bubonic plague. In fact, the playhouses were closed twice during Shakespeare's lifetime as a result of outbreaks of the plague. Because of the hostile atmosphere created by the civil authorities, playhouses were typically built outside the city limits in order to place them beyond the jurisdiction of authorities.

Interior of the Swan Theatre—from a pen and ink drawing made in 1596 (Mansell Collection)

When The Lord Chamberlain's Men (the troupe to which Shakespeare belonged), first began performing, *The Theater*, owned by Richard and Cuthbert Burbage, was their theatrical home. Constructed in 1576 just outside the city limits of London, *The Theater* was the first of the public playhouses. Plays had previously been performed in England in the square- or rectangular-shaped yards of the inns where traveling bands of actors stayed, but this arrangement had a serious drawback—it was far too easy for customers to enter and leave the grounds without paying the price of admission. Playhouses like *The Theater* were therefore a significant improvement since the enclosed design made it possible to have a single opening where tickets could be taken from those entering.

The Chamberlain's Men were financially successful, but a problem arose in 1598 concerning the property on which *The Theater* stood. The owner of the property planned to have the playhouse torn down once the lease on the land expired, so in late 1598 the Chamberlain's Men dismantled the building and reassembled it a short distance from the south bank of the River Thames, renaming it *The Globe*.

In 1603, The Lord Chamberlain's Men regrouped under the patronage of King James I and took the name The King's Men; the shareholders were thenceforward considered to be members of the royal household. Unfortunately, the company's fortunes took a downturn in 1613 when, during a performance of *Henry VIII*, a cannon was fired, setting the thatched roof of *The Globe* ablaze. Within an hour, the building was destroyed.

The King's Men rebuilt the playhouse, and the new *The Globe* theater, completed in 1614, was circular in shape. The "wooden O" (as it is referred to in *Henry V*) of *The Globe* actually had twenty sides, with an outer diameter of about one hundred yards. Some historians have estimated that it could hold up to three thousand people, but others dispute that figure as being far too high.

Playbills would be posted around the city to advertise for new plays, but due to the fact that the roofs of "public" theaters such as *The Globe* were open to the elements, plays could be performed only in daylight and in good weather. The theatrical company would fly a flag from the roof of the building to notify people if a performance was to proceed. If, however, the flag was not flown, theatergoers would be spared an unnecessary trip.

Those attending a play paid the gatekeeper at the entrance. In addition to standing room around the stage, seats were available in the three tiers of the gallery which encircled the playhouse. For the price of one penny (about sixty cents today), the "groundlings," as they were called, gained admission to the pit. Those who could afford to do so paid for gallery seating; the lowest tier was the least expensive, with the price climbing to as high as one shilling (about seven dollars today) for seats in the uppermost tier. The roof shielded the patrons seated in the galleries either from the heat of the sun or, in case the weather turned bad, from a sudden downpour.

Plays typically had a theatrical run of ten performances, although, depending on the popularity of the piece, some were performed up to about sixteen times; less popular plays, however, might have only six performances. The performances proceeded without intermission and usually took about two hours, although a number of Shakespeare's plays run significantly longer. When the play was about to begin, a trumpet would sound three times.

Shakespeare's plays were performed on what is referred to as a "thrust" stage; it was about five feet high and measured $27\frac{1}{2}$ feet deep by 43 feet wide; it probably sloped downward at the front (downstage) and projected out into the pit. The stage was covered by a roof (referred to as "the heavens"), which was painted to resemble a starlit sky upon which the signs of the zodiac were depicted. The area beneath the stage was referred to as "hell"; a trapdoor in the floor of the stage allowed for the entrances and exits of ghosts, monsters, and devils.

There was no scenery, nor was there a curtain that could be closed at the end of scenes or acts, so playwrights used the lines spoken by the actors to set the scene and to indicate when a scene or act was ending. A rhyming couplet, for example, would often indicate the conclusion of a scene. The gallery directly behind the stage was used for scenes in which actors were required to be either in an upper story of a house, on the battlements of a castle, or in some other elevated position. Musicians and even spectators also occupied the gallery.

At the rear of the stage (upstage) was the "tiring house" where the actors dressed (attired themselves). The tiring house had two or three doors providing access to the stage. Even though many of the plays performed were set in earlier times, the actors did not wear period costumes; the period in which a play was set would merely be suggested by certain period touches in the costumes, such as spears or helmets. Consequently, a play such as *Julius Caesar* which was set around 44 B.C.E. would have been performed in the current fashions of Elizabethan England. However, despite being historically inaccurate, the costumes the actors wore were quite lavish and were therefore not a disappointment to the audience.

Since it was illegal for women to perform in public at that time, boys or young men played the women's roles in the plays. Often, in order for a boy actor to be tall enough to be convincing in the role of an adult woman, he had to wear chopines (wooden platforms strapped to the soles of the shoes); the long skirts, which were fashionable, hid the chopines from view. Because of the restriction on women performing, Shakespeare's plays had few female characters, and, in many of his plays, the heroine would spend much of the play disguised as a boy.

The plays of Shakespeare were of course crucial to the success of the company, but the troupe also had the most renowned actor of the time, Richard Burbage. Burbage was the first actor to portray Hamlet. Although Shakespeare was himself an actor, he is only known to have performed secondary roles.

Other noted actors in the troupe were William Kempe, a comedian, and Robert Asmin, a singer and dancer, both of whom were also shareholders in The King's Men. The average size for a theatrical company was twenty-five members, about half of whom would usually be shareholders. Other actors were employed part-time as needed.

Because actors in Shakespeare's time needed to project their voices for open-air performances, they tended to employ a more exaggerated, declamatory style of acting than would be acceptable to today's audiences. Some actors went to extremes, however. Shakespearean scholars generally agree that Hamlet's instruction to the Players not to "tear a passion . . . to very rags" reflects his views on the tendency to overact amongst his contemporaries. Shakespeare's presence during rehearsals of his plays would have given him the opportunity to personally instruct an actor in the way a line should be delivered.

His Verse

Although Shakespeare's dramatic output alone would have been sufficient to ensure his place among English writers, his reputation as an author does not rest solely upon his plays. He wrote poetry, as well, including the erotic narrative poems *Venus and Adonis* (1593) and *The Rape of Lucrece* (1594). He also composed 154 *Sonnets*, which were circulated in manuscript prior to their publication in 1609.

Shakespeare's poetic output was not confined to his poems, however. At the beginning of Shakespeare's career as a playwright, the prevailing style for dialog was rhyming couplets (that is, two succeeding lines of poetry that rhyme), so a high percentage of the lines in his earlier plays rhyme. In one of his early works, *Love's Labor's Lost*, for example, nearly half of the lines rhyme.

As time passed, however, Shakespeare used fewer rhymed couplets for dialog and began favoring blank verse for his plays. Blank verse consists of unrhymed lines of iambic pentameter; iambic pentameter is the technical term for lines ten syllables in length with alternating stresses (that is, an unstressed syllable followed by a stressed syllable). Although Shakespeare continued to use rhyming couplets in his plays when he wanted to indicate the end of a scene or when the situation might call for a more artificial style of speech, he favored a much more naturalistic form of expression in his later plays.

Even in his early plays, however, Shakespeare was outdoing his fellow playwrights. For example, because of the prevailing style of rhyming couplets, most of the characters in a play would sound the same; in other words, one character's "voice" could not be distinguished from that of another. In contrast, even early on Shakespeare's characters each spoke with a recognizable voice. Even without the speaker's identity being revealed, no one would have any difficulty distinguishing the innocent yet passionate utterances of Juliet from the prosaic vulgarity of her Nurse. Furthermore, if, during the course of a play, a character underwent a significant change, Shakespeare would indicate this change by altering the character's speech patterns. One example of this technique is Othello who begins to sound more and more like Iago as he becomes progressively more infected with the "pestilence" Iago pours into his ear.

Shakespeare also used speech patterns to indicate a character's social rank. In his plays, members of the nobility usually speak in blank verse, while those of lower station speak in prose, reflecting their limited education. Shakespeare also uses prose to indicate when the more highly ranked characters are speaking informally or are under stress.

Another one of the many noteworthy aspects of Shakespeare's technique is his use of setting to reinforce ideas in his plays. In *Antony and Cleopatra*, for example, the cold austerity of Rome reflects the emotional coldness and sterility of the Romans, whereas the sun-drenched setting of Egypt reflects the passionate love of the title characters.

Furthermore, Shakespeare used imagery not only to create atmosphere but also to convey themes. *Hamlet*, for example, contains numerous references to disease and decay, reinforcing the theme of the moral and political rot in Denmark. In addition to demonstrating his technical brilliance, Shakespeare's works reveal insights into human nature that none of his predecessors or contemporaries could begin to approach.

Shakespeare's technique and contributions to drama and literature place him at the pinnacle of his art. It's no surprise then that each succeeding generation sees new additions to the ranks of "Bardolators."

The Taming of the Shrew

Date

The Taming of the Shrew was initially published in 1623 in the First Folio, but most scholars believe that it was written between 1590 and 1594. They think this because a similar play called *The Taming of a Shrew* (note the slight difference in the titles) was published anonymously in 1594. Although the relationship of the two plays has been the subject of considerable debate over the years, most experts now agree that *The Taming of the Shrew* was written first and that *A Shrew* probably was a "memorial recreation" of Shakespeare's play, that is, a version of the play based on a reconstruction from memory by someone who had either seen *The Shrew* or performed in it. Although the main plot of *A Shrew* is structurally similar to *The Shrew,* there are many differences between the two plays, and the dialog in *A Shrew* is significantly inferior to that of Shakespeare's play.

Sources

There are three separate sources for the various plot strands of *The Taming of the Shrew.* The source for the main plot concerning Katherina and Petruchio is not entirely clear. At one time, scholars thought that there was an earlier version of the play that was the source for both *The Shrew* and *A Shrew.* However, that theory has now been rejected by most experts in favor of the theory mentioned in the "Date" section above. There are, in fact, many possible sources for the taming plot. Not only do many early Roman comedies include shrewish wives, but English drama does as well. For example, Noah's wife in some medieval mystery plays refuses to obey her husband and get into the ark even though the floodwaters are rising. Because of similarities in wording between *The Taming of the Shrew* and an old ballad called

"A Merry Jest of a Shrewd and Curst Wife Lapped in Morel's Skin for Her Good Behavior" (ca.1550), it seems likely that Shakespeare was familiar either with this poem or a similar one. These ballads promoted the idea that physical violence was the best means for dealing with a shrewish wife. In the case of "The Merry Jest," the wife is beaten until she is bleeding and then is wrapped in the salted hide of a dead horse until she agrees to be obedient to her husband.

Unlike the complicated situation of the source for the plot of the taming of Katherina, the source for the one concerning Bianca and Lucentio is clear. It was derived from George Gascoigne's *Supposes* (1566), which is an adaptation of *I Suppositi* (1509) by Ariosto. The plot was not, however, original to Ariosto in that it is structurally similar to the Roman comedies of Plautus and Terence. In Gascoigne's version, Polynesta (the character who is parallel to Bianca) is pregnant by her lover Erostrato. Erostrato changes places with his servant Dulipo, who helps his master to defeat a rich but elderly rival. Gascoigne's version also includes the unexpected arrival of Erostrato's father, who discovers to his horror that Dulipo is impersonating Erostrato and that a stranger is impersonating him.

The plot involving the duping of Christopher Sly in the Induction is similar to a story in *The Arabian Nights* (collected ca.1450), in which Harun al-Rashid tricks Abu Hassan. The Duke of Burgundy, Philip the Good (1396–1467), once played the trick on a drunken man after having heard the story, possibly from an ambassador from the East. The story of this incident was passed along, eventually appearing in *De rebus burgundicis* (1584) by Hueterus. Scholars believe that this may have been Shakespeare's source for the Christopher Sly plot, although it is also possible that a collection of stories, now lost, by Richard Edwards was Shakespeare's source for the Induction scene. Interestingly, in *A Shrew*, the Sly plot is not abandoned early in the play as it is in *The Shrew*. In *A Shrew*, Christopher Sly remains on stage, commenting on what he is viewing throughout much of the play. Eventually, he falls asleep as a result of the amount of alcohol he has consumed. When he awakens at the end of the play, Sly is convinced that his experience as a "lord" has been nothing more than a vivid dream; in at least one version, he intends to go home to his wife and try out the taming methods he has just witnessed. Although some experts think that similar scenes may have originally been included in Shakespeare's version, there is no actual evidence that such was the case.

Text

The Taming of the Shrew was first published in the First Folio Edition of 1623. This text is considered by scholars to be authoritative, and all subsequent editions have been published with only minor textual differences.

The Taming of the Shrew

Original Text and Modern Version

Cast of Characters:

Induction:

Lord	wealthy nobleman
Christopher Sly	tinker (a person who mends old pots and pans)
Hostess	owner of the tavern
Page	servant to Lord
Players	traveling actors who are hired to put on a play
Huntsmen, Servants, Messenger	

****

Baptista Minola	rich gentleman of Padua
Katherina	Baptista's elder daughter (the "shrew")
Bianca	Baptista's younger daughter
Petruchio	suitor to Katherina
Lucentio	suitor to Bianca; son of Vincentio
Gremio	rich old man who is another suitor to Bianca
Hortensio	suitor to Bianca
Vincentio	wealthy merchant who is the father of Lucentio
Tranio	servant to Lucentio
Biondello	servant to Lucentio
Grumio	servant to Petruchio
Curtis	servant to Petruchio
Peter	a servant
Pedant	schoolmaster who masquerades as Vincentio
Widow	woman who eventually marries Hortensio
Tailor	
Haberdasher	peddler of small goods
Servants	

Synopsis

Induction

Scene 1

Before an alehouse on a heath.

Enter beggar, **Christophero Sly**, *and* **Hostess**.

Sly   I'll pheeze you, in faith.

Hostess   A pair of stocks, you rogue!

Sly   Y' are a baggage, the Slys are no rogues.
Look in the chronicles; we came in with Richard
Conqueror. Therefore *paucas pallabris*; let the world
6   slide. Sessa!

Hostess   You will not pay for the glasses you have
burst?

Sly   No, not a denier. Go by, Saint Jeronimy! go
10   to thy cold bed, and warm thee.

Hostess   I know my remedy; I must go fetch the
[thirdborough].

[*Exit.*]

Sly   Third, or fourth, or fifth borough, I'll answer
him by law. I'll not budge an inch, boy; let him come,
15   and kindly.

Falls asleep.

Wind Horns. Enter a **Lord** *from hunting, with his* **Train**.

Induction

Scene 1

In front of a tavern in the English countryside.

[**Hostess** *and* **Sly** *enter, arguing.*]

Sly   [*with drunken belligerence*] I'll let you have it, for sure!

Hostess   I'll have you put in the stocks, you villain!

Sly   You whore, the Slys aren't villains! Look in the record books! We came over with Richard the Conqueror. So just shut up and forget about it. Drop it. [*He is trying to sound important, meaning to refer to William the Conqueror, but he's either too drunk or too ignorant to get his facts right.*]

Hostess   [*indignantly*] So you won't pay for the glasses you've broken?

Sly   No, not one penny. Go away, Saint Jeronimy! Go to your cold bed and pleasure yourself. [*In trying to sound more educated than he is, he misquotes* The Spanish Tragedy, *a play by Thomas Kyd which contains the line,* "Hieronimo, beware! Go by, go by!"]

Hostess   I know my rights! I'm going to get a police officer! [**Hostess** *storms out.*]

Sly   [*shouting after her*] Bring any officer you like; I'll defend myself in court to him. I'm not going anywhere, by God! He's welcome to come.

[**Sly** *lies down on the ground and falls asleep.*]

[*Hunting horns sound in the distance. A* **Lord** *and his* **servants** *enter.*]

27

Lord   Huntsman, I charge thee, tender well my hounds
   (Brach Merriman, the poor cur, is emboss'd),
   And couple Clowder with the deep-mouth'd brach.
   Saw'st thou not, boy, how Silver made it good
20 At the hedge-corner, in the coldest fault?
   I would not lose the dog for twenty pound.

First Huntsman   Why, Belman is as good as he, my lord;
   He cried upon it at the merest loss,
   And twice to-day pick'd out the dullest scent.
25 Trust me, I take him for the better dog.

Lord   Thou art a fool; if Echo were as fleet,
   I would esteem him worth a dozen such.
   But sup them well and look unto them all:
   To-morrow I intend to hunt again.

30 **First Huntsman**   I will, my lord.

Lord   What's here? One dead, or drunk? See, doth
   he breathe?

Second Huntsman   He breathes, my lord. Were he not
      warm'd with ale,
   This were a bed but cold to sleep so soundly.

Lord   O monstrous beast, how like a swine he lies!
   Grim death, how foul and loathsome is thine image!
36 Sirs, I will practice on this drunken man.
   What think you, if he were convey'd to bed,
   Wrapp'd in sweet clothes, rings put upon his fingers,
   A most delicious banquet by his bed,
40 And brave attendants near him when he wakes,
   Would not the beggar then forget himself?

Lord   [*speaking to* **First Huntsman**] Huntsman, I order you to see to it that my hounds are well taken care of. Let Merriman, poor dog, breathe; she's foaming at the mouth from exhaustion. And tie Clowder up with the deep-voiced bitch. [*with enthusiasm*] Did you see, fellow, how Silver kept going at the boundary hedge where the scent was almost nonexistent? I would rather lose twenty pounds than lose that dog. [*The pound is a unit of British currency.*]

First Huntsman   Why, Belman is just as good a dog as he is, my lord. He kept baying even when the scent was almost lost and twice today was the one to pick up the faintest scent. Believe me, I think he's the better dog.

Lord   [*disagreeing, but goodnaturedly*] You're a fool. If Echo were as fast as Belman, I would consider him to be worth a dozen of him. But feed them and attend to them all. I plan to hunt again tomorrow.

First Huntsman   I will, my lord.

Lord   [*suddenly seeing* **Sly**] But what's this? A corpse or a drunk? See if he's breathing.

Second Huntsman   He's breathing, my lord. This would be a very cold bed for him to be sleeping so soundly on if he weren't warmed by all the ale he's had to drink.

Lord   [*in great disgust*] What a disgusting beast, lying there like a pig!

[*speaking as if death is a person*] Grim Death, what a horrid and revolting sight is sleep because it resembles you so!

[*to his servants*] Men, I'm going to play a trick on this drunken man. Tell me, if he were carried to a bed, dressed in clean clothes, with expensive rings put on his fingers, a delicious meal at his bedside, and uniformed servants standing by when he awakes, would this beggar then forget who he really is?

29

First Huntsman   Believe me, lord, I think he cannot
choose.

Second Huntsman   It would seem strange unto him when he
wak'd.

Lord   Even as a flatt'ring dream or worthless fancy.
45   Then take him up and manage well the jest.
Carry him gently to my fairest chamber,
And hang it round with all my wanton pictures.
Balm his foul head in warm distilled waters,
And burn sweet wood to make the lodging sweet.
50   Procure me music ready when he wakes,
To make a dulcet and a heavenly sound;
And if he chance to speak, be ready straight,
And with a low submissive reverence
Say, "What is it your honour will command?"
55   Let one attend him with a silver basin
Full of rose-water and bestrew'd with flowers,
Another bear the ewer, the third a diaper,
And say, "Will't please your lordship cool your hands?"
Some one be ready with a costly suit,
60   And ask him what apparel he will wear;
Another tell him of his hounds and horse,
And that his lady mourns at his disease.
Persuade him that he hath been lunatic,
And when he says he is, say that he dreams,
65   For he is nothing but a mighty lord.
This do, and do it kindly, gentle sirs;
It will be pastime passing excellent,
If it be husbanded with modesty.

First Huntsman   My lord, I warrant you we will play our
part,
70   As he shall think by our true diligence
He is no less than what we say he is.

First Huntsman   Believe me, my lord, I think he would have no choice but to do so.

Second Huntsman   It will seem very strange to him when he wakes up.

Lord   Just like a sweet dream or impossible fantasy. Pick him up and do a good job of carrying out the joke. Carry him carefully to my finest room and hang my best pictures on the walls. Wash his disgusting head with warm, scented water and burn fragrant wood to perfume the room. I want you to have musicians ready to play sweet, heavenly music when he awakes, and if he happens to speak to you, immediately answer him with great reverence and say, "What would your honor command us to do?" One of you must wait on him with a silver washbasin full of rosewater and strewn with flowers, a second carry the pitcher, and the third a cloth, and say, "Would your lordship like to cool your hands?" Someone have an expensive suit of clothing ready and ask him what he wants to wear. Another one tell him about his hounds and his horse. And say that his wife is grief-stricken over his disease; persuade him that he has been insane, and if he says that he must now be mad, say that he is mistaken, for he is and always has been a powerful nobleman. Do this and if you can do it convincingly, gentlemen, it will be an excellent joke, assuming that you can maintain your self-control.

First Huntsman   My lord, I promise you that, because of our faithfulness to perform our roles, he will be convinced by our actions that he is nothing less than what we say he is.

Lord   Take him up gently and to bed with him,
And each one to his office when he wakes.

[Some bear out Sly.] Sound trumpets.

Sirrah, go see what trumpet 'tis that sounds.

[Exit Servingman.]

75   Belike some noble gentleman that means
(Travelling some journey) to repose him here.

Enter **Servingman**.

How now? who is it?

Servant   An't please your honor, players
That offer service to your lordship.

Enter **Players**.

Lord   Bid them come near.
Now, fellows, you are welcome.

80 **Players**   We thank your honor.

Lord   Do you intend to stay with me to-night?

2nd Player   So please your lordship to accept our duty.

Lord   With all my heart. This fellow I remember
Since once he play'd a farmer's eldest son.
85   'Twas where you woo'd the gentlewoman so well.
I have forgot your name; but, sure, that part
Was aptly fitted and naturally perform'd.

Lord   Pick him up gently and put him to bed. And, when he wakes, let each of you wait on him as you would when performing your duties to me.

[*Several **Servants** carry **Sly** out. A trumpet sounds offstage.*]

Lord   [*to a remaining servant*] Go see why that trumpet is sounding, fellow.

[**Servant** *bows to* **Lord** *and exits.*]

[*to himself*] I suppose it's some nobleman on a journey who intends to rest at my home.

[**Servant** *returns.*]

Well, who is it?

Servant   My Lord, it's a traveling troupe of actors who are offering to perform for your lordship.

Lord   Tell them to come here.

[*The **Players** enter.*]

Now, men, you are welcome here.

Players   We thank you, your honor.

Lord   [*graciously*] Do you intend to spend the night at my residence?

A Player   If your lordship will allow us to earn our lodging by performing for you.

Lord   Most definitely. [*pointing to one of the players*] I remember this fellow from when he played a farmer's eldest son; it was where you wooed the noble lady so well. I've forgotten your name, but that part was certainly well suited to you, and you performed it well.

1st Player   I think 'twas Soto that your honor means.

Lord   'Tis very true; thou didst it excellent.
90   Well, you are come to me in a happy time,
The rather for I have some sport in hand.
Wherein your cunning can assist me much.
There is a lord will hear you play to-night;
But I am doubtful of your modesties,
95   Lest, over-eyeing of his odd behavior,
(For yet his honor never heard a play),
You break into some merry passion,
And so offend him; for I tell you, sirs,
If you should smile, he grows impatient.

100   **1st Player**   Fear not, my lord, we can contain ourselves,
Were he the veriest antic in the world.

Lord   Go, sirrah, take them to the buttery,
And give them friendly welcome every one.
Let them want nothing that my house affords.

Exit one with the Players

A Player   I think your honor means Soto. [*He probably refers to a character in* Women Pleased, *a play by Jacobean playwright John Fletcher.*]

Lord   That's it! You did it excellently well. Well, you've arrived at a good time for me, particularly since I have some entertainment planned in which your skill can greatly help me. There is a nobleman who will watch your performance tonight, but I'm concerned, when you see his strange behavior—for he has never seen a play before—that you might burst out laughing and so offend him. For I warn you, men, that if you show your amusement, he will become angry.

A Player   Don't worry, my lord. We could control ourselves even if he were the oddest person in the world.

Lord   [*to* **Servant**] You, fellow, take them to the pantry [*to give them something to eat and drink*] and give them all a warm welcome. Let them lack nothing that my house can offer.

[*One* **Servant** *leaves with the* **Players.**]

105   Sirrah, go you to Barthol'mew my page,
       And see him dress'd in all suits like a lady;
       That done, conduct him to the drunkard's chamber,
       And call him madam, do him obeisance.
       Tell him from me, as he will win my love,
110   He bear himself with honorable action,
       Such as he hath observ'd in noble ladies
       Unto their lords, by them accomplished;
       Such duty to the drunkard let him do,
       With soft low tongue and lowly courtesy,
115   And say, "What is't your honor will command,
       Wherein your lady, and your humble wife,
       May show her duty and make known her love?"
       And then with kind embracements, tempting kisses,
       And with declining head into his bosom,
120   Bid him shed tears, as being overjoyed
       To see her noble lord restor'd to health,
       Who for this seven years hath esteem'd him
       No better than a poor and loathsome beggar.
       And if the boy have not a woman's gift
125   To rain a shower of commanded tears,
       An onion will do well for such a shift,
       Which in a napkin (being close convey'd)
       Shall in despite enforce a watery eye.
       See this dispatch'd with all the haste thou canst;
130   Anon I'll give thee more instructions.

Exit a Servingman.

Lord   [*to another* **Servant**] Lad, go find Bartholomew, my
page, and see that he dresses up like a lady. When you've
done that, take him to the drunkard's room and call him
"madam" and bow to him. Tell Bartholomew that I said, if
he wishes to gain my approval, he must behave himself
with great dignity, the way he has seen noble ladies behave
toward their husbands. Tell him to act in such a way toward
the drunkard, speaking to him in soft, gentle tones and with
submissive courtesy, saying, "What does your honor
command, so that your humble lady-wife may show you
her obedience and love?" And then, with loving embraces,
tempting kisses, and with her head resting on the drunkard's chest, tell Bartholomew to weep as if overjoyed to see
her noble husband, who for seven years had thought
himself no better than a poor and repulsive beggar,
restored to health. And if Bartholomew isn't able to cry like
a woman, tell him to carry an onion in wrapped in a napkin,
which will do the trick to help him fake his tears. See to it
that all this is carried out as quickly as you can. I'll give you
more instructions soon.

[**Servant** *bows to* **Lord** *and exits.*]

I know the boy will well usurp the grace,
Voice, gait, and action of a gentlewoman.
I long to hear him call the drunkard husband,
And how my men will stay themselves from laughter
135   When they do homage to this simple peasant.
I'll in to counsel them; haply my presence
May well abate the over-merry spleen,
Which otherwise would grow into extremes.

[*Exeunt.*]

Scene 2

Enter aloft the drunkard [**Sly**] *with* **Attendants**, *some with apparel, basin and ewer, and other appurtenances; and* **Lord**.

Sly   For God's sake, a pot of small ale.

1st Servingman   Will't please your [lordship] drink a cup of sack?

2nd Servingman   Will't please your honor taste of these conserves?

3rd Servingman   What raiment will your honor wear to-day?

I know that Bartholomew will successfully imitate the gracefulness, voice, walk, and movements of a gentle-woman. I can't wait to hear him call the drunkard "husband" and watch my men hide their laughter when they treat this simple peasant with great respect. I'll go in to advise them. Perhaps my presence will help them master their desire to laugh which they might not otherwise be able to control.

[*All those still present leave.*]

Scene 2

A bedchamber in the **Lord's** *house.*

[**Sly** *enters balcony area of stage, accompanied by* **Servants,** *some carrying clothing, others with the silver basin, pitcher, and so on. The* **Lord** *also enters.*]

Sly For God's sake, get me a mug of weak ale.

First Servant Would your lordship like a glass of imported wine?

Second Servant Would your honor like to taste these fruit confections?

Third Servant What clothing will your honor wear today?

5 **Sly**   I am Christophero Sly, call not me honor
nor lordship. I ne'er drank sack in my life; and
if you give me any conserves, give me conserves of
beef. Ne'er ask me what raiment I'll wear, for
I have no more doublets than backs, no more stock-
10   ings than legs, nor no more shoes than feet–
nay, sometime more feet than shoes, or such shoes
as my toes look through the overleather.

Lord   Heaven cease this idle humor in your honor!
O, that a mighty man of such descent,
15   Of such possessions and so high esteem,
Should be infused with so foul a spirit!

Sly   What, would you make me mad? Am not
I Christopher Sly, old Sly's son of Burton-heath,
by birth a pedlar, by education a card-maker, by
20   transmutation a bear-herd, and now by present
profession a tinker? Ask Marian Hacket, the fat
ale-wife of Wincot, if she know me not. If she say
I am not fourteen pence on the score for sheer ale,
score me up for the lying'st knave in Christendom.
25   What! I am not bestraught: Here's–

3rd Servingman   O, this it is that makes your lady mourn!

2nd Servingman   O, this is it that makes your servants
droop!

Sly   [*impatiently*] I am Christopher Sly. Don't call me "honor" or "lordship." I've never drunk imported wine in my life, and if you give me food, give me some dried beef. Don't ask me what clothing I will wear, for I have no more jackets than I have backs, no more socks than I have legs, no more shoes than I have feet. In fact, sometimes I have more feet than I have shoes to put on them, or when I do have shoes, my toes are likely to be sticking out through the leather.

Lord   May heaven end this foolish mood in your honor! Oh, how dreadful that a powerful man of such noble birth, with so many possessions and such a fine reputation, should be possessed by so terrible an illness!

Sly   [*with growing exasperation*] What, are you trying to drive me insane? Am I not Christopher Sly, old Sly's son of Burtonheath, by birth a peddler, trained to be a maker of combing tools for wool, changed to a bear-keeper, and currently a tinker? Go ask Marian Hacket, the fat female innkeeper of Wincot whether or not she knows me. If she doesn't say that I owe her fourteen pence for ale alone, you may call me the worst liar in Christendom. What! I am not insane! Here's—

Third Servant   [*interrupts*] Oh, this is what makes your lady mourn!

Second Servant   Oh, this is what makes your servants so sad!

Lord   Hence comes it that your kindred shuns your house,
As beaten hence by your strange lunacy.
30   O noble lord, bethink thee of thy birth,
Call home thy ancient thoughts from banishment,
And banish hence these abject lowly dreams.
Look how thy servants do attend on thee,
34   Each in his office ready at thy beck.
Wilt thou have music? Hark! Apollo plays,

Music.

And twenty caged nightingales do sing.
Or wilt thou sleep? We'll have thee to a couch,
Softer and sweeter than the lustful bed
On purpose trimm'd up for Semiramis.
40   Say thou wilt walk; we will bestrew the ground.
Or wilt thou ride? Thy horses shall be trapp'd,
Their harness studded all with gold and pearl.
Dost thou love hawking? Thou hast hawks will soar
Above the morning lark. Or wilt thou hunt?
45   Thy hounds shall make the welkin answer them
And fetch shrill echoes from the hollow earth.

1st Servingman   Say thou wilt course, thy greyhounds
are as swift
As breathed stags; ay, fleeter than the roe.

2nd Servingman   Dost thou love pictures? We will fetch
thee straight
50   Adonis painted by a running brook,
And Cytherea all in sedges hid,
Which seem to move and wanton with her breath,
Even as the waving sedges play with wind.

Lord   This is what causes your family to avoid your house, as if chased away by your strange madness. Oh, noble lord, remember your lineage, bring back your previous memories from exile and cast out these fantasies of being a common man. See how your servants stand ready to serve you, each one ready to perform his duties at your command. Would you like to have music? Listen! Apollo plays. [*Apollo was the god of music.*]

[*Music plays.*]

And twenty caged nightingales sing for you. Or would you rather sleep? We'll bring you to a bed that is softer and more fragrant than the bed prepared for Semiramis, the lusty queen of Assyria. If you prefer to take a walk, we will prepare your path. Or would you like to ride? Your horses shall be fitted out with harnesses studded with gold and pearls. Do you wish to go hawking? You have hawks that will soar higher than the morning lark. Or would you like to hunt? Your hounds will bark loudly enough to make the heavens answer them and cause the depths of the earth to echo their cries.

First Servant   If you choose to hunt with your hounds, your greyhounds are as fast as stags with stamina to spare, yes, even faster than the deer.

Second Servant   Do you love pictures? We will immediately bring a painting of Adonis by a brook, with Cytherea hiding in the rushes which are so realistically depicted that they seem to move and tremble with desire while she breathes, like the wind playing with the rushes. [*Adonis was a handsome prince who was pursued by Cytherea, also called Venus.*]

Lord   We'll show thee Io as she was a maid,
55   And how she was beguiled and surpris'd,
As lively painted as the deed was done.

3rd Servingman   Or Daphne roaming through a thorny
wood,
Scratching her legs that one shall swear she bleeds,
And at that sight shall sad Apollo weep,
60   So workmanly the blood and tears are drawn.

Lord   Thou art a lord, and nothing but a lord.
Thou hast a lady far more beautiful
Than any woman in this waning age.

1st Servingman   And till the tears that she hath shed for
thee
65   Like envious floods o'errun her lovely face,
She was the fairest creature in the world,
And yet she is inferior to none.

Sly   Am I a lord, and have I such a lady?
Or do I dream? Or have I dream'd till now?
70   I do not sleep: I see, I hear, I speak;
I smell sweet savors, and I feel soft things.
Upon my life, I am a lord indeed,
And not a tinker, nor Christopher Sly.
Well, bring our lady hither to our sight,
75   And once again a pot o' th' smallest ale.

2nd Servingman   Will't please your mightiness to wash
your hands?
O how we joy to see your wit restor'd!
O that once more you knew but what you are!
These fifteen years you have been in a dream,
80   Or when you wak'd, so wak'd as if you slept.

Sly   These fifteen years! by my fay, a goodly nap,
But did I never speak of all that time?

Lord   We'll show you a painting of the virgin Io who was seduced and taken by surprise by Zeus. It's so lifelike that it looks as if it were really happening. [*Io was a beautiful young woman who was loved by Zeus. Out of jealousy, Zeus' wife changed Io into a cow.*]

Third Servant   Or one of Daphne wandering through a thorny forest, scratching her legs so that one would swear she actually bleeds. So convincingly are her blood and tears painted that sad Apollo would weep at the sight. [*Daphne was a nymph who was changed into a laurel tree by Diana, the virgin goddess of the hunt, to protect her from attempted rape by the god Apollo.*]

Lord   You are a lord, and nothing but a lord. You have a noble wife who is far more beautiful than any other woman in this corrupt time.

First Servant   And until the tears she has wept for you drowned her face like floodwaters envious of her beauty, she was the loveliest creature in the world. Yet even now there is no one more beautiful than she.

Sly   [*suddenly dropping his protestations*] Am I a lord? And do I have such a wife? Or am I dreaming? Or was I dreaming until now? I'm not asleep. I see, I hear, I speak, I smell sweet odors, and I feel soft things. I swear that I must be a lord indeed and not a tinker or Christopher Sly. Well, bring my lady-wife here. And be sure to bring me a mug of ale.

Second Servant   Would your mightiness like to wash his hands? Oh, how happy we are to see your sanity restored! Oh, that you might once again fully know who you are! For the past fifteen years you have been like one in a dream, or when you awakened, it was as if you still slept.

Sly   [*in amazement*] For fifteen years? By God, that was quite a nap. But didn't I ever speak during that time?

1st Servingman O yes, my lord, but very idle words,
For though you lay here in this goodly chamber,
85   Yet would you say ye were beaten out of door,
And rail upon the hostess of the house,
And say you would present her at the leet,
Because she brought stone jugs and no seal'd quarts.
Sometimes you would call out for Cicely Hacket.

90 **Sly** Ay, the woman's maid of the house.

3rd Servingman Why, sir, you know no house nor no such maid,
Nor no such men as you have reckon'd up,
As Stephen Sly, and old John Naps of Greece,
And Peter Turph, and Henry Pimpernell,
95   And twenty more such names and men as these,
Which never were, nor no man ever saw.

Sly Now Lord be thanked for my good amends!

All Amen.

Enter [the **Page** *as a] lady, with* **Attendants**.

Sly I thank thee, thou shalt not lose by it.

100 **Page** How fares my noble lord?

Sly Marry, I fare well, for here is cheer enough.
Where is my wife?

Page Here, noble lord, what is thy will with her?

Sly Are you my wife and will not call me husband?
My men should call me "lord"; I am your goodman.

106 **Page** My husband and my lord, my lord and husband,
I am your wife in all obedience.

First Servant   Oh, yes, my lord, but only things that made no sense. For even though you lay here in this splendid room, you would say that you were being violently thrown out of a tavern and shout at the proprietress of the place, and say that you would take her to court because she had brought you watered-down jugs of ale and not sealed quarts. Sometimes you would call out for Cicely Hacket.

Sly   Ah, yes, the landlady's maid.

Third Servant   Why, sir, you don't know of any such tavern or maid. Nor do you know any men such as you have named: Stephen Sly, or old John Naps of Greece, or Peter Turph and Henry Pimpernell, and twenty other such men which don't exist, nor has anyone ever seen them.

Sly   Thank God for my recovery!

All   Amen.

Sly   [*to all*] I thank you. You shall not lose out because of my illness.

[*The* **Page**, *dressed as a lady, enters with attendants.*]

Page   [*speaking in a high-pitched voice*] How are you, my noble lord?

Sly   Indeed, I do well for I have all that I want to eat and drink. Where is my wife?

Page   [*bowing to indicate that he is* **Sly's** *wife*] Here I am, my lord. What do you want of me?

Sly   If you are my wife, why do you not call me "husband"? My servants should call me "lord," but I am your husband.

Page   You are my husband as well as my lord, my lord *and* husband. I am your obedient wife in all things.

47

Sly   I know it well. What must I call her?

Lord   Madam.

110 **Sly**   Al'ce madam, or Joan madam?

Lord   Madam, and nothing else, so lords call
ladies.

Sly   Madam wife, they say that I have dream'd,
And slept above some fifteen year or more.

Page   Ay, and the time seems thirty unto me,
115   Being all this time abandon'd from your bed.

Sly   'Tis much. Servants, leave me and her alone.
Madam, undress you, and come now to bed.

Page   Thrice noble lord, let me entreat of you
To pardon me yet for a night or two;
120   Or, if not so, until the sun be set.
For your physicians have expressly charg'd,
In peril to incur your former malady,
That I should yet absent me from your bed.
124   I hope this reason stands for my excuse.

Sly   Ay, it stands so that I may hardly tarry so
long. But I would be loath to fall into my dreams
again. I will therefore tarry in despite of the flesh
and the blood.

Enter a **Messenger**.

Sly I know that.

[*Not knowing the correct etiquette, he asks the others present for instruction.*] What should I call her?

Lord "Madam."

Sly "Madam Alice"? Or "Madam Joan"?

Lord Just "madam." That's how noblemen address their wives.

Sly Madam wife, they say that I have been dreaming or asleep for more than fifteen years.

Page Yes, and it has seemed as if it were thirty years to me, having all this time been banished from your bed.

Sly That's a long time. Servants, leave my wife and me alone. Now, madam, undress and come to bed.

Page [*thinking quickly*] Thrice-noble lord, let me beg you to excuse me for a night or two more, or, if not, at least until the sun sets, for your physicians have explicitly ordered, at risk of your former illness recurring, that I should continue to refrain from sleeping with you. I hope my excuse will stand as a valid excuse.

Sly [*regretfully*] Oh, yes, it stands so that I can hardly bear the delay. [*He refers to his penis.*] But I would certainly not want to fall into my dreams again, so I will wait despite the desires raging in my flesh and blood.

[*A **Messenger** enters.*]

Messenger   Your honor's players, hearing your amendment,
130   Are come to play a pleasant comedy,
For so your doctors hold it very meet,
Seeing too much sadness hath congeal'd your blood,
And melancholy is the nurse of frenzy.
Therefore they thought it good you hear a play,
135   And frame your mind to mirth and merriment,
Which bars a thousand harms and lengthens life.

Sly   Marry, I will, let them play it. Is not a
comonty a Christmas gambold, or a tumbling-trick?

Page   No, my good lord, it is more pleasing stuff.

140 **Sly**   What, household stuff?

Page   It is a kind of history.

Sly   Well, we'll see't. Come, madam wife, sit by
my side, and let the world slip, we shall ne'er be
younger.

[*They all sit.*] *Flourish.*

Messenger   Your honor's actors, hearing of your recovery, have come to perform a pleasant comedy. For your doctors consider it very appropriate, seeing that too much sadness has thickened your blood, and sorrow is the cause of madness. Therefore, they thought you should hear a play and thus direct your thoughts to laughter and amusement, which prevent a thousand maladies and promote long life. [*"Thickened blood" was a common medical diagnosis of the time.*]

Sly   Indeed, I will do so. Let them perform it. But is a "comonty" a Christmas gambold or a tumbling trick. [*He mispronounces both "comedy" and "gambol." A gambol is a lively dance.*]

Page   No, my good lord. This is more enjoyable stuff.

Sly   What, household stuff? [**Sly** *is punning on a phrase meaning sexual activity between spouses.*]

Page   [*ignoring* **Sly's** *double entendre*] It is a sort of story.

Sly   Well, let's see it. Come, madam wife, sit next to me and let the world drift past. We're not getting any younger.

[*They all sit down to watch the play. Trumpets sound to signal that it's about to begin.*]

Act one

Scene 1

*Enter **Lucentio** and his man **Tranio**.*

Lucentio   Tranio, since for the great desire I had
    To see fair Padua, nursery of arts,
    I am arriv'd for fruitful Lombardy,
    The pleasant garden of great Italy,
5   And by my father's love and leave am arm'd
    With his good will and thy good company,
    My trusty servant, well approv'd in all,
    Here let us breathe, and haply institute
    A course of learning and ingenious studies.
10   Pisa, renowned for grave citizens,
    Gave me my being and my father first,
    A merchant of great traffic through the world,
    Vincentio come of Bentivolii;
    Vincentio's son brought up in Florence,
15   It shall become to serve all hopes conceiv'd,
    To deck his fortune with his virtuous deeds.
    And therefore, Tranio, for the time I study,
    Virtue and that part of philosophy
    Will I apply that treats of happiness
20   By virtue specially to be achiev'd.
    Tell me thy mind, for I have Pisa left
    And am to Padua come, as he that leaves
    A shallow plash to plunge him in the deep,
    And with society seeks to quench his thirst.

Act one

Scene 1

A bustling public street in Padua.

[**Lucentio** *and his servant* **Tranio** *enter.*]

Lucentio   [*with great enthusiasm*] Tranio, because I had such a great longing to see beautiful Padua, birthplace of learning [*Padua was famed throughout Europe for its university*], I have come here on my way to fertile Lombardy, that pleasant garden of great Italy. And my father has given his loving permission to do so, providing me with his approval and your delightful companionship, my trustworthy servant, dependable in all you do. Let us break our journey here for a while and begin a delightful course of learning and intellectual studies.

Pisa, famous for its worthy citizens, was my birthplace as well as my father's before me, Vincentio, a man of great success in the business world and the son of Bentivolii. I was raised in Florence, and it is only right that I should try to further enhance his reputation by living in such a way as to fulfill his hopes for me. And therefore, Tranio, while I study here, I will gladly do my very best to be virtuous and studious.

Tell me your opinion, for I have left Pisa and am here in Padua, much like someone who has climbed out of a shallow pool in order to dive into deep waters to fully satisfy his thirst.

25 **Tranio**   *Mi perdonato*, gentle master mine;
        I am, in all affected as yourself,
        Glad that you thus continue your resolve
        To suck the sweets of sweet philosophy.
        Only, good master, while we do admire
30   This virtue and this moral discipline,
        Let's be no Stoics nor no stocks, I pray,
        Or so devote to Aristotle's checks
        As Ovid be an outcast quite abjur'd.
        Balk logic with acquaintance that you have,
35   And practice rhetoric in your common talk,
        Music and poesy use to quicken you,
        The mathematics, and the metaphysics,
        Fall to them as you find your stomach serves you:
        No profit grows where is no pleasure ta'en.
40   In brief, sir, study what you most affect.

    Lucentio   Gramercies, Tranio, well dost thou advise.
        If, Biondello, thou wert come ashore,
        We could at once put us in readiness,
        And take a lodging fit to entertain
45   Such friends as time in Padua shall beget.
        But stay a while, what company is this?

    Tranio   Master, some show to welcome us to town.

    Enter **Baptista** *with his two daughters,* **Katherina** *and*
    Bianca, **Gremio**, *a pantaloon,* **Hortensio**, [*suitor*] *to*
    Bianca. **Lucentio**, **Tranio** *stand by.*

Tranio   [*hesitantly*] I beg your pardon, my dear master; I feel exactly as you do. I am glad that you are so determined to drink deeply of the sweet waters of knowledge. Yet, good master, although I admire your virtue and self-control, please let's not be Stoics or as emotionless as blocks of wood. Nor should we be so devoted to Aristotle's stern ethics that Ovid [*a love poet*] becomes a despised outcast. Practice your debating skills with your acquaintances and your verbal skills in your everyday conversations, but use music and poetry to refresh yourself; "eat up" mathematics and physics as much as you want to satisfy your appetite for learning, but you will not benefit from your studies if you take no time to relax. In other words, sir, let your "appetite" either for study or for pleasure determine what you do.

Lucentio   Many thanks, Tranio, your advice is good. If only Biondello had come ashore here, we could begin at once to prepare ourselves and find a place to stay that would be suitable for entertaining whatever friends we shall make while in Padua. [*Shakespeare refers incorrectly to Padua, an inland city, as having a coastline harbor.*]

[**Lucentio's** *attention is caught by an approaching noisy crowd.*]

But wait a moment. Who are all these people?

Tranio   [*guessing*] Some group sent to welcome us to town, master.

[**Baptista, Katherina, Bianca, Gremio,** *and* **Hortensio** *enter.* **Lucentio and Tranio** *stand watching.*]

Baptista   Gentlemen, importune me no farther,
For how I firmly am resolv'd you know:
50   That is, not to bestow my youngest daughter
Before I have a husband for the elder.
If either of you both love Katharina,
Because I know you well, and love you well,
Leave shall you have to court her at your pleasure.

Gremio   To cart her rather; she's too rough for me.
56   There, there, Hortensio, will you any wife?

Katherina   [*To Baptista.*] I pray you, sir, is it your will
To make a stale of me amongst these mates?

Hortensio   Mates, maid, how mean you that? No mates
for you,
60   Unless you were of gentler, milder mould.

Katherina   I' faith, sir, you shall never need to fear.
Iwis it is not half way to her heart;
But if it were, doubt not her care should be
To comb your noddle with a three-legg'd stool,
65   And paint your face, and use you like a fool.

Hortensio   From all such devils, good Lord deliver us!

Baptista   [*to* **Gremio** *and* **Hortensio**] Gentlemen, stop pleading with me, for you know how firmly determined I am not to give my younger daughter to anyone before I have a husband for the elder. Because I know both of you and love you both well, if either of you love Katherina, you will have my permission to court her as much as you wish.

Gremio   [*to himself*] You mean to cart her; she's too rough for me. [*He refers to the practice of shaming disorderly women or prostitutes by driving them through the streets in a cart to be ridiculed.*]

[*mockingly, to* **Hortensio**] There, there, Hortensio, will you marry anyone at all? [*He's implying that* **Hortensio** *should consider himself lucky if anyone at all would agree to marry him.*]

Katherina   [*furiously, to* **Baptista**] Tell me, sir, are you trying to make a whore of me in front of these prospective "husbands"? [*Her use of the word "stale," another word for prostitutes, may show that she overheard* **Gremio's** *rude remark.*]

Hortensio   [*mockingly, to* **Katherina**] Husbands, missy! What do you mean by that? There will be no husband for you unless you conform by being more docile and calm.

Katherina   [*returning his mockery*] Believe me, sir, you needn't be afraid. It isn't even close to what I want, but if it were, I would show my great love for you by beating your empty head with a three-legged stool, painting your face with your own blood, and treating you like the clown that you are.

Hortensio   May the good Lord protect us from such devils as you!

Gremio   And me too, good Lord!

Tranio   Husht, master, here's some good pastime
toward;
That wench is stark mad or wonderful froward.

70 **Lucentio**   But in the other's silence do I see
Maid's mild behavior and sobriety.
Peace, Tranio!

Tranio   Well said, master, mum, and gaze your fill.

Baptista   Gentlemen, that I may soon make good
75 What I have said, Bianca, get you in,
And let it not displease thee, good Bianca,
For I will love thee ne'er the less, my girl.

Katherina   A pretty peat! it is best
Put finger in the eye, and she knew why.

80 **Bianca**   Sister, content you in my discontent.
Sir, to your pleasure humbly I subscribe;
My books and instruments shall be my company,
On them to look and practice by myself.

Lucentio   Hark, Tranio, thou mayst hear Minerva speak.

85 **Hortensio**   Signior Baptista, will you be so strange?
Sorry am I that our good will effects
Bianca's grief.

Gremio   And me too, good Lord!

Tranio   [*to* **Lucentio**] Hush, master! Right here is some good entertainment. That young woman is either insane or amazingly headstrong.

Lucentio   [*entranced by* **Bianca**] But in the other's silence I see the gentle behavior and modesty of the ideal maiden. Quiet, Tranio!

Tranio   [*approvingly*] That's right, master; hush! and look all you want.

Baptista   Gentlemen, so that I may do as I have said—

[*He turns here and speaks tenderly to his younger daughter*] Bianca, go inside, and don't let it upset you, dear Bianca, for, even so, I love you, my child.

Katherina   [*scornfully*] Pretty little daddy's pet! She can force herself to weep any time she can come up with a reason.

Bianca   [*bursting into tears, to* **Katherina's** *disgust*] Sister, be happy in my unhappiness.

[*turning to speak to her father*] Sir, I humbly submit to your wishes. My books and musical instruments will keep me company, and I will study them and practice in solitude.

Lucentio   [*even more infatuated with* **Bianca**] Listen, Tranio! When she speaks, it's as if Minerva herself is speaking. [*Minerva was the Roman goddess of wisdom.*]

Hortensio   Signior Baptista, must you be so unnatural a father? I am sorry that our [*referring to himself and* **Gremio**] attentions have caused Bianca's sorrow.

Gremio   Why will you mew her up,
Signior Baptista, for this fiend of hell,
And make her bear the penance of her tongue?

90 **Baptista**   Gentlemen, content ye; I am resolv'd.
Go in, Bianca.

[*Exit Bianca.*]

And for I know she taketh most delight
In music, instruments, and poetry,
Schoolmasters will I keep within my house,
95   Fit to instruct her youth. If you, Hortensio,
Or, Signior Gremio, you, know any such,
Prefer them hither; for to cunning men
I will be very kind, and liberal
To mine own children in good bringing-up,
100 And so farewell. Katherina, you may stay,
For I have more to commune with Bianca.

Exit

Katherina   Why, and I trust I may go too, may I not?
What, shall I be appointed hours, as though (belike)
I knew not what to take and what to leave? Ha!

Exit

Gremio   [*plaintively*] Why do you lock her away, Signior
Baptista, for the sake of this fiend of hell [**Katherina**], and
make her endure the abusive things she says to her?

Baptista   Gentlemen, that is enough. I am determined.

[*gently, to* **Bianca**] Go inside, Bianca.

[**Bianca** *leaves.*]

[*to* **Hortensio** *and* **Gremio**] And because I know that she
loves music, instruments, and poetry, I will hire capable
tutors to live in my home to instruct her. If you, Hortensio,
or you, Signior Gremio, know of any, send them here, for I
will be very kind to such skilful men, and generous to
ensure the proper education for my own children. And so,
goodbye.

[*to* **Katherina**] Katherina, you may stay here, for I have
more I want to discuss with Bianca.

[**Baptista** *leaves.*]

Katherina   [*indignantly*] Why, and I hope that I may come,
too, may I not? What, must I make an appointment with
you, as if I didn't know what was or was not worthwhile?
Ha!

[*She laughs in disgust and leaves.*]

Gremio   You may go to the devil's dam; your gifts
106   are so good, here's none will hold you. Their
love is not so great, Hortensio, but we may blow our
nails together, and fast it fairly out. Our cake's
dough on both sides. Farewell; yet for the love
I bear my sweet Bianca, if I can by any means light
on a fit man to teach her that wherein she delights,
112   I will wish him to her father.

Hortensio   So will I, Signior Gremio. But a word, I
pray. Though the nature of our quarrel yet never
brook'd parle, know now upon advice, it toucheth
us both, that we may yet again have access to our
fair mistress, and be happy rivals in Bianca's love,
118   to labor and effect one thing specially.

Gremio   What's that, I pray?

Hortensio   Marry, sir, to get a husband for her sister.

121   **Gremio**   A husband! a devil.

Hortensio   I say, a husband.

Gremio   I say, a devil. Think'st thou, Hortensio,
though her father be very rich, any man is so very
125   a fool to be married to hell?

Gremio   [*sarcastically, to the now-absent* **Katherina**] You may go to the devil's mother [*a common curse*]; you have so many good qualities that no one here will keep you from leaving.

[*to* **Hortensio**] The love of women is not so important to us, Hortensio, that we would not more willingly twiddle our thumbs to pass the time and go without their company. Both our plans have collapsed like a cake that has fallen. Goodbye. Yet because of the love I have for my sweet Bianca, if I can somehow find a qualified man to teach her the subjects she loves, I will recommend him to her father.

Hortensio   [*with resignation*] So will I, Signior Gremio. But one more thing, please. Although our rivalry has previously prevented us from getting along, as I now think things over I realize that it would benefit us both to join forces; thus we may once more be able to be with our beautiful young lady and be happy rivals for Bianca's love if we work together to accomplish one particular thing.

Gremio   And what would that be?

Hortensio   [*lowering his voice and looking around to make sure he is not overheard*] Actually, sir, to get a husband for her sister.

Gremio   [*astounded*] A husband! You must mean a devil!

Hortensio   I mean a husband.

Gremio   [*insistently*] I say a devil! Do you really think, Hortensio, that, even though her father is very rich, any man would be such a fool as to marry a hellion?

Hortensio   Tush, Gremio; though it pass your patience
and mine to endure her loud alarums, why, man,
there be good fellows in the world, and a man could
light on them, would take her with all faults, and
130   money enough.

Gremio   I cannot tell; but I had as lief take her
dowry with this condition: to be whipt at the high
cross every morning.

Hortensio   Faith, as you say, there's small choice
135   in rotten apples. But come, since this bar in
law makes us friends, it shall be so far forth friendly
maintain'd till by helping Baptista's eldest daughter
to a husband we set his youngest free for a husband,
and then have to't afresh. Sweet Bianca, happy man
be his dole! He that runs fastest gets the ring. How
141   say you, Signior Gremio?

Gremio   I am agreed, and would I had given him the
best horse in Padua to begin his wooing that would
thoroughly woo her, wed her, and bed her, and rid
145   the house of her! Come on.

Exeunt ambo [Gremio and Hortensio]. Manent
Tranio and Lucentio.

Tranio   I pray, sir, tell me, is it possible
That love should of a sudden take such hold?

Hortensio   Come now, Gremio, although her loud outbursts would be more than either your patience or mine could stand, why, sir, there are good men in this world, if a person could only find them, that would be willing to take her even with all her faults [*for a moment, his confidence seems shaken, but then he continues determinedly*] if there were enough money involved.

Gremio   I don't know about that, but I would rather be pub-licly whipped every morning to get her dowry than to be married to her.

Hortensio   [*sighing*] You're right; it's like choosing between rotten apples. But come, since this difficult obstacle causes us to be allies, we must remain friends until, by helping Baptista's older daughter get a husband, we free his younger one to get a husband as well, and then we'll resume our competition.

Sweet Bianca, the man who wins you will be happy indeed. He who runs fastest gets the ring. [*He refers to the sport of catching a ring on the tip of a lance, and making a pun on "wedding ring."*]

What do you think, Signior Gremio?

Gremio   I agree, and I wish that I could give the man who would be willing to woo Katherina the best horse in Padua so that he could completely woo her, marry her, sleep with her, and get her out of the house! Come on.

[**Gremio** *and* **Hortensio** *leave together.* **Lucentio** *and* **Tranio** *remain.*]

Tranio   [*seeing his master's love-struck expression*] Tell me please, sir, is it possible to fall in love so suddenly?

Lucentio   O Tranio, till I found it to be true,
I never thought it possible or likely.
150 But see, while idly I stood looking on,
I found the effect of love in idleness,
And now in plainness do confess to thee,
That art to me as secret and as dear
As Anna to the queen of Carthage was:
155 Tranio, I burn, I pine, I perish, Tranio,
If I achieve not this young modest girl.
Counsel me, Tranio, for I know thou canst;
Assist me, Tranio, for I know thou wilt.

Tranio   Master, it is no time to chide you now,
160 Affection is not rated from the heart.
If love have touch'd you, nought remains but so,
"Redime te captum quam queas minimo."

Lucentio   Gramercies, lad. Go forward, this contents;
The rest will comfort, for thy counsel's sound.

Tranio   Master, you look'd so longly on the maid,
166 Perhaps you mark'd not what's the pith of all.

Lucentio   O yes, I saw sweet beauty in her face,
Such as the daughter of Agenor had,
That made great Jove to humble him to her hand,
When with his knees he kiss'd the Cretan strond.

171 **Tranio**   Saw you no more? Mark'd you not how her sister
Began to scold, and raise up such a storm
That mortal ears might hardly endure the din?

Lucentio   [*in awe*] Oh, Tranio, until it happened to me, I
never believed it to be possible or even probable. But look,
while I stood idly watching, love-in-idleness cast its spell on
me, and now I freely admit it to you, who are as trusted and
close to me as Anna was to her sister Dido, the Queen of
Carthage. Tranio, I burn, I suffer, I die, Tranio, if I cannot
win the love of this gentle young girl! Advise me, Tranio,
for I know you can; help me, Tranio, for I know you will.
[*Love-in-idleness was a flower which was believed to cause
people to fall in love with the next living thing they saw.
See* A Midsummer Night's Dream, 2.1.165–172.]

Tranio   Master, now is not the time to scold you; scolding
can't drive love out of the heart. If love has touched you,
there is nothing to be said except this: "Ransom yourself
from captivity for the smallest possible price."

Lucentio   Many thanks, good fellow. Go on, I'm satisfied.
Whatever else you have to say will cheer me, for your
advice is good.

Tranio   Master, you were looking so intently at the maiden
that perhaps you didn't notice what the heart of the matter
is.

Lucentio   Oh yes, I saw such sweet beauty in her face as the
daughter of Agenor had, that made the great Jove humble
himself to win her when he went down on his knees on the
shores of Crete. [*In mythology, Europa, the daughter of
Agenor, was loved by the Roman god Jupiter, who transformed himself into a bull and carried her off.*]

Tranio   Didn't you see anything else? Didn't you notice how
her sister began to scold and carry on so that human ears
could hardly stand the uproar?

Lucentio   Tranio, I saw her coral lips to move,
And with her breath she did perfume the air.
Sacred and sweet was all I saw in her.

Tranio   Nay, then 'tis time to stir him from his trance.
I pray, awake, sir; if you love the maid,
Bend thoughts and wits to achieve her. Thus it stands:
180   Her elder sister is so curst and shrewd
That till the father rid his hands of her,
Master, your love must live a maid at home,
And therefore has he closely mew'd her up,
Because she will not be annoy'd with suitors.

185 **Lucentio**   Ah, Tranio, what a cruel father's he!
But art thou not advis'd, he took some care
To get her cunning schoolmasters to instruct her?

Tranio   Ay, marry, am I, sir; and now 'tis plotted.

Lucentio   I have it, Tranio.

Tranio   Master, for my hand,
190   Both our inventions meet and jump in one.

Lucentio   Tell me thine first.

Tranio   You will be schoolmaster,
And undertake the teaching of the maid:
That's your device.

Lucentio   It is; may it be done?

Tranio   Not possible; for who shall bear your part,
195   And be in Padua here Vincentio's son,
Keep house and ply his book, welcome his friends,
Visit his countrymen and banquet them?

Lucentio   [*still speaking of* **Bianca**] Tranio, I saw her coral lips move, and her sweet breath perfumed the air. All that I saw in her was blessed and sweet.

Tranio   [*to himself and/or the audience*] It's time to wake him from his spell.

[*more loudly, to* **Lucentio**] Please, sir, wake up. If you love the girl, set your thoughts and mind on how to win her. Here is the situation: Her elder sister is so horrible and ill-natured that until their father gets her off his hands, master, your beloved must continue to live unmarried at home, and, therefore, he has confined her to home so that she won't be bothered by suitors.

Lucentio   [*shocked out of his daydreams about* **Bianca**] Ah, Tranio, what an unkind father he is! [*suddenly struck by inspiration*] But aren't you aware that he has resolved to hire skillful instructors to teach her?

Tranio   Yes indeed, I am, sir, and now we have a plan.

Lucentio   I've got it, Tranio!

Tranio   Master, I'll bet we both have the same plan in mind.

Lucentio   [*eagerly*] Tell me yours first.

Tranio   You will be an instructor and will hire yourself out to teach the young lady. That's your strategy.

Lucentio   It is. [*anxiously*] Do you think it will work?

Tranio   [*momentarily discouraged*] It's not possible. For who will perform your role as Vincentio's son here in Padua, and live in your lodgings and study your books, greet your friends, visit your fellow countrymen and entertain them?

Lucentio   *Basta,* content thee; for I have it full.
　　　　We have not yet been seen in any house,
200　　Nor can we be distinguish'd by our faces
　　　　For man or master. Then it follows thus:
　　　　Thou shalt be master, Tranio, in my stead;
　　　　Keep house and port and servants, as I should.
　　　　I will some other be, some Florentine,
205　　Some Neapolitan, or meaner man of Pisa.
　　　　'Tis hatch'd and shall be so. Tranio, at once
　　　　Uncase thee; take my colour'd hat and cloak.
　　　　When Biondello comes, he waits on thee,
　　　　But I will charm him first to keep his tongue.

210 **Tranio**   So had you need.
　　　　In brief, sir, sith it your pleasure is,
　　　　And I am tied to be obedient—
　　　　For so your father charg'd me at our parting;
　　　　"Be serviceable to my son," quoth he,
215　　Although I think 'twas in another sense—
　　　　I am content to be Lucentio,
　　　　Because so well I love Lucentio.

Lucentio   Tranio, be so, because Lucentio loves,
219　　And let me be a slave, t' achieve that maid
　　　　Whose sudden sight hath thrall'd my wounded eye.

　　　　Enter **Biondello**.

　　　　Here comes the rogue. Sirrah, where have you been?

Biondello   Where have I been? Nay, how now, where
　　　　are you? Master, has my fellow Tranio stol'n your
　　　　clothes? Or you stol'n his? or both? Pray what's
225　　the news?

Lucentio   [*excitedly*] That's okay; don't worry. I have it all figured out. We haven't yet visited any houses, nor can anyone tell by looking at our faces which of us is servant and which is master. So here's what we'll do: You will be the master, Tranio, in my place, take lodgings, live in high style, employ servants, all just as I would do. I will be someone else, someone from Florence or Naples or some unimportant man from Pisa. I've figured it all out, and that's how it shall be. Hurry, Tranio, take off what you're wearing. Take my expensive hat and cloak. [*They exchange garments as he speaks.*] When Biondello arrives, he will be your servant. But I must make sure he keeps quiet about it.

Tranio   You had better do so. To be brief, sir, since you want to do this, and I am required to obey you—for that's what your father ordered me to do when we left, saying, "Be sure to obey my son," although I don't think he meant it in this way—I am willing to be Lucentio, since I love Lucentio.

Lucentio   Tranio, that's what you must be because I, Lucentio, am in love. And let me be a slave in order to win that girl, whose appearance has enslaved my wounded glance.

[**Biondello** *arrives.*]

Here comes the rascal.

[*to* **Biondello**] Fellow, where have you been?

Biondello   [*startled to see how* **Lucentio** *and* **Tranio** *are dressed*] Where have I been? No, really, where are you?

[*to* **Lucentio**] Master, has my fellow servant Tranio stolen your clothes? Or have you stolen his? Or both? [*looking from one to the other in utter confusion*] Tell me, what's going on?

Lucentio   Sirrah, come hither, 'tis no time to jest,
And therefore frame your manners to the time.
Your fellow Tranio here, to save my life,
Puts my apparel and my count'nance on,
230   And I for my escape have put on his;
For in a quarrel since I came ashore
I kill'd a man, and fear I was descried.
Wait you on him, I charge you, as becomes,
While I make way from hence to save my life.
You understand me?

235 **Biondello**   Ay, sir!—[*aside*] ne'er a whit.

Lucentio   And not a jot of Tranio in your mouth,
Tranio is chang'd into Lucentio.

Biondello   The better for him, would I were so too!

Tranio   So could I, faith, boy, to have the next wish after,
240   That Lucentio indeed had Baptista's youngest daughter.
But, sirrah, not for my sake, but your master's, I advise
You use your manners discreetly in all kind of companies.
When I am alone, why then I am Tranio;
But in all places else [your] master Lucentio.

245 **Lucentio**   Tranio, let's go.
One thing more rests, that thyself execute—
To make one among these wooers. If thou ask me why,
Sufficeth, my reasons are both good and weighty.

Exeunt.

The Presenters above speaks.

1st Servingman   My lord, you nod, you do not mind the
play.

Lucentio   [*whispering to* **Biondello**] Fellow, come here. This is no time to make jokes, so therefore behave according to circumstances. In order to save my life, your fellow servant Tranio here is wearing my clothes and pretending to be me, and I, in order to escape, have put on his. I killed a man in a quarrel since I landed, and I'm afraid I was seen. I order you to wait on him as you would wait on me, while I escape from here to save my life. Do you understand me?

Biondello   Yes, sir! [*to himself*] Not one bit.

Lucentio   And don't even mention Tranio. Tranio has become Lucentio.

Biondello   [*enviously*] All the better for him. I wish I were him, too!

Tranio   So would I, for certain, boy, in order to have the next wish come true: That Lucentio really had Baptista's younger daughter. But, fellow, for your master's sake and not for mine, I advise you to behave prudently whenever we are with others. When I am alone, then I am Tranio, but anywhere else, I am your master, Lucentio.

Lucentio   Tranio, let's go. There's one more thing to be done, and you must do it—You must become one of Bianca's suitors. If you want to know why, let's just say that I have reasons that are both good and compelling.

*The actors from the **Induction** speak.*

First Servant   [*to* **Sly**] My lord, you're falling asleep. You aren't watching the play.

Sly   Yes, by Saint Anne, do I. A good matter,
251   surely: comes there any more of it?

Page   My lord, 'tis but begun.

Sly   'Tis a very excellent piece of work, madam
lady; would 'twere done!

They sit and mark.

Scene 2

Enter **Petruchio** *and his man* **Grumio**.

Petruchio   Verona, for a while I take my leave
To see my friends in Padua, but of all
My best beloved and approved friend,
Hortensio; and I trow this is his house.
5   Here, sirrah Grumio, knock, I say.

Grumio   Knock, sir? whom should I knock? Is there
any man has rebus'd your worship?

Petruchio   Villain, I say, knock me here soundly.

Grumio   Knock you here, sir? Why, sir, what am I,
10   sir, that I should knock you here, sir?

Petruchio   Villain, I say, knock me at this gate,
And rap me well, or I'll knock your knave's pate.

Sly   Yes, by Saint Anne [*a common oath*], I am. It's a very good play, indeed. Is there any more of it?

Page   [*still masquerading as* **Sly's** *wife*] My lord, it's just begun.

Sly   It's a very excellent play, madam lady. [*muttering to himself*] I wish it were over!

[*They continue to sit and watch the play.*]

Scene 2

In front of **Hortensio's** *house in Padua.*

[**Petruchio** *and his servant* **Grumio** *arrive in Padua.*]

Petruchio   For a time, Verona, I will leave you in order to see my friends in Padua, but especially my dearest and best friend, Hortensio. And I believe this is his house. Here, Grumio, I order you to knock. [**Petruchio** *is from Verona.*]

Grumio   [*startled*] Knock, sir? Whom shall I knock? Has someone insulted your worship? [*He thinks* **Petruchio** *is ordering him to hit someone rather than to knock on the door.*]

Petruchio   Fool, I tell you to knock me vigorously here! [*He means that* **Grumio** *should knock on the gate for him.*]

Grumio   Knock you here, sir! Why, sir, who am I that I should knock you here, sir?

Petruchio   [*growing increasingly angry*] Idiot, I tell you to knock me at this gate and strike me well, or I'll knock your stupid head!

Grumio   My master is grown quarrelsome. I should
    knock you first,
And then I know after who comes by the worst.

15 **Petruchio**   Will it not be?
Faith, sirrah, and you'll not knock, I'll ring it.
I'll try how you can *sol, fa,* and sing it.

He wrings him by the ears.

Grumio   Help, [masters], help, my master is mad.

Petruchio   Now knock when I bid you, sirrah villain!

Enter **Hortensio.**

20 **Hortensio**   How now, what's the matter? My old
friend Grumio! and my good friend Petruchio!
How do you all at Verona?

Petruchio   Signior Hortensio, come you to part the fray?
24 *Con tutto [il] core, ben trovato,* may I say.

Hortensio   *Alla nostra casa ben venuto, molto honorato
signor mio Petruchio.*
Rise, Grumio, rise, we will compound this quarrel.

Grumio   My master, you have grown quarrelsome. If I knock
you first, I know who will end up with the worst of the
bargain. [*He means that he will be in trouble if he does
what he believes* **Petruchio** *is ordering him to do.*]

Petruchio   [*roaring in indignation at* **Grumio's** *disobedience*] You disobey me? Indeed, fellow, if you won't knock,
I will ring it. [*He puns on "ring," like a bell, as opposed to
"wring," meaning to twist or squeeze.*] I'll see how you *sol*,
fa, and sing it.

[**Petruchio** *wrings* **Grumio** *by the ears.*]

Grumio   [*howling in pain*] Help, gentlemen, help! My master
is insane!

Petruchio   Now, knock when I tell you to, you scoundrel!

[**Hortensio** *arrives.*]

Hortensio   [*shocked to see* **Petruchio** *and* **Grumio** *scuf-
fling*] What is this? What's the matter? My old friend
Grumio! And my good friend Petruchio! How is everyone
in Verona?

Petruchio   Signior Hortensio, have you come to break up
the fight? [*in Italian*] With all my heart I tell you that I am
glad to see you. [*He lets go of* **Grumio**, *who falls to the
ground, holding his ears.*]

Hortensio   [*in Italian*] Welcome to my house, my honored
friend Petruchio. Get up, Grumio, get up. Let us settle this
quarrel.

Grumio   Nay, 'tis no matter, sir, what he 'leges in
Latin. If this be not a lawful cause for me to leave
30   his service, look you, sir. He bid me knock
him and rap him soundly, sir. Well, was it fit for a
servant to use his master so, being perhaps (for
aught I see) two and thirty, a peep out?
Whom would to God I had well knock'd at first,
35   Then had not Grumio come by the worst.

Petruchio   A senseless villain! Good Hortensio,
I bade the rascal knock upon your gate,
And could not get him for my heart to do it.

Grumio   Knock at the gate? O heavens! Spake
40   you not these words plain, "Sirrah, knock me
here; rap me here; knock me well, and knock me
soundly"? And come you now with "knocking at
the gate"?

Petruchio   Sirrah, be gone, or talk not, I advise you.

Hortensio   Petruchio, patience, I am Grumio's pledge.
46   Why, this' a heavy chance 'twixt him and you,
Your ancient, trusty, pleasant servant Grumio.
And tell me now, sweet friend, what happy gale
Blows you to Padua here from old Verona?

Petruchio   Such wind as scatters young men through the
50   world
To seek their fortunes farther than at home,
Where small experience grows. But in a few,
Signior Hortensio, thus it stands with me:
Antonio, my father, is deceas'd,
55   And I have thrust myself into this maze,
Happily to wive and thrive as best I may.
Crowns in my purse I have, and goods at home,
And so am come abroad to see the world.

Grumio   No, it doesn't matter, sir, what he says in Latin. [*An uneducated man, he doesn't realize that they were speaking Italian.*] You will see, sir, whether or not this gives me legal cause to stop working for him. He ordered me to knock him and hit him vigorously, sir. Well, was it right for a servant to treat his master in such a way, since I can see that he's too old for me to fight and drunk besides? But I wish to God that I *had* knocked him hard, sir, for then I would not have had the worst of it.

Petruchio   [*in disgust*] What a stupid fool! Good friend Hortensio, I ordered the scoundrel to knock on your gate and couldn't for the life of me get him to do it.

Grumio   [*shocked to hear what his master says*] Knock at the gate! For heaven's sake! Didn't you plainly say these words, "Fool, knock me here, strike me here, knock me well and knock me vigorously"? And now you claim it was "knocking at the gate"?

Petruchio   Fellow, either leave or be silent, I warn you.

Hortensio   Calm down, Petruchio. I will defend him to you. Why, this is a sad quarrel between him, your faithful and trustworthy servant Grumio, and you. Now tell me, my dear friend, what fortunate wind blows you here to Padua from old Verona?

Petruchio   The kind of wind that scatters young men across the world to seek their fortunes at places other than home, a place where little experience can be gained. But, to be brief, Signior Hortensio, this is how it is with me: My father, Antonio, has died, and I have plunged into this labyrinth of life to get happily married and to succeed as well as I can. I have money in my pocket and possessions at home, and so I have set off to see the world.

Hortensio   Petruchio, shall I then come roundly to thee,
60   And wish thee to a shrewd ill-favor'd wife?
Thou'dst thank me but a little for my counsel;
And yet I'll promise thee she shall be rich;
And very rich. But th' art too much my friend,
And I'll not wish thee to her.

Petruchio   Signior Hortensio, 'twixt such friends as we
66   Few words suffice; and therefore, if thou know
One rich enough to be Petruchio's wife
(As wealth is burthen of my wooing dance),
Be she as foul as was Florentius' love,
70   As old as Sibyl, and as curst and shrowd
As Socrates' Xantippe, or a worse,
She moves me not, or not removes at least
Affection's edge in me. [Whe'er] she is as rough
As are the swelling Adriatic seas,
75   I come to wive it wealthily in Padua;
If wealthily, then happily in Padua.

Grumio   Nay, look you, sir, he tells you flatly what
his mind is. Why, give him gold enough, and marry
him to a puppet or an aglet-baby, or an old trot with
80   ne'er a tooth in her head, though she have as many
diseases as two and fifty horses. Why, nothing comes
amiss, so money comes withal.

Hortensio   Petruchio, may I speak plainly and tell you where to find yourself a nasty, shrewish wife? You probably won't be grateful for my advice, but I can assure you that she is rich, very rich indeed. But you're too good a friend for me to do that to you, and I won't wish her on you.

Petruchio   Signior Hortensio, good friends such as we are understand one another with very few words spoken. Therefore, if you know someone rich enough to be Petruchio's wife—since wealth is the main refrain of my wooing dance—even if she is an ugly hag like the woman Florentius loved, or as ancient as Sibyl, and just as bad-tempered and shrewish as Socrates' wife, Xanthippe, or even worse than any of them, she doesn't bother me, nor will she dull my affection for her even if she be as rough as the tempestuous Adriatic sea. I've come to Padua to get a rich wife, and if she be rich, then I will be content in Padua. [*Florentius was a legendary knight betrothed to an ugly old woman. Upon his agreeing to be ruled by her, she was transformed into a beautiful young girl. Sibyl was the prophetess to whom the god Apollo gave as many years of life as the grains of sand she could hold in her hand. Xanthippe was a woman reputed to have been very shrewish.*]

Grumio   [*in response to* **Hortensio's** *dubious expression*] No, listen, sir, he's telling you exactly what he thinks. Why, give him enough gold and marry him to a puppet or a lifeless doll or even to a toothless old whore—even one with as many diseases as you might find in fifty-two horses— why, as long as there's enough money in the bargain, nothing else matters.

Hortensio   Petruchio, since we are stepp'd thus far in,
I will continue that I broach'd in jest.
85   I can, Petruchio, help thee to a wife
With wealth enough, and young and beauteous,
Brought up as best becomes a gentlewoman.
Her only fault, and that is faults enough,
Is that she is intolerable curst
90   And shrowd and froward, so beyond all measure,
That were my state far worser than it is,
I would not wed her for a mine of gold.

Petruchio   Hortensio, peace! thou know'st not gold's effect.
Tell me her father's name and 'tis enough;
95   For I will board her, though she chide as loud
As thunder when the clouds in autumn crack.

Hortensio   Her father is Baptista Minola,
An affable and courteous gentleman.
Her name is Katherina Minola,
100   Renown'd in Padua for her scolding tongue.

Petruchio   I know her father, though I know not her,
And he knew my deceased father well.
I will not sleep, Hortensio, till I see her,
And therefore let me be thus bold with you
105   To give you over at this first encounter,
Unless you will accompany me thither.

Grumio   I pray you, sir, let him go while the humor
lasts. A' my word, and she knew him as well as I do,
she would think scolding would do little good upon
110   him. She may perhaps call him half a score
knaves or so. Why, that's nothing; and he begin
once, he'll rail in his rope-tricks. I'll tell you what,
sir, and she stand him but a little, he will throw a
figure in her face, and so disfigure her with it, that she
shall have no more eyes to see withal than a cat.
116   You know him not, sir.

Hortensio   Petruchio, since we've said this much, I'll go on
even though when I began speaking, I was just joking. I can,
Petruchio, help you get a wife who is quite wealthy, not to
mention being young and beautiful, as well as having been
brought up in a manner appropriate to a noblewoman.
[*hesitantly*] Her only shortcoming—and quite a shortcoming it is—is that she is so unbelievably bad-tempered and
shrewish and obstinate that even if I were poverty-stricken
I would not marry her for an entire goldmine.

Petruchio   Hortensio, hush! You don't know how powerful
an incentive gold is. Just tell me her father's name, for I will
woo her even though she should scold as loudly as thunder
when the autumn clouds collide.

Hortensio   Her father is Baptista Minola, a pleasant and
well-mannered gentleman. Her name is Katherina Minola,
famous throughout Padua for her scolding tongue.

Petruchio   I know her father (although I don't know her),
and he knew my deceased father well. [*with decision*] I
won't sleep, Hortensio, until I see her. And therefore let me
be so bold as to take my leave of you, unless you want to
come along with me.

Grumio   [*to* **Hortensio**] Please, sir, let him go while he's in
the mood to do so. I swear, if she knew him as well as I do,
she would know that scolding will have little effect upon
him. She may call him ten nasty names if she chooses, but
that will be nothing to him. Once he starts in, he'll rattle out
his rope-tricks. [*He mispronounces "rhetoric," meaning that*
Petruchio's *cleverness with words will completely defeat*
her.] Let me tell you, sir, if she tries to resist him, he will
throw a figure of speech at her and so humiliate her that
she won't be able to see any better than a blind cat. You
don't know him, sir.

Hortensio   Tarry, Petruchio, I must go with thee,
For in Baptista's keep my treasure is.
He hath the jewel of my life in hold,
His youngest daughter, beautiful Bianca,
120

And her withholds from me [and] other more,
Suitors to her and rivals in my love;
Supposing it a thing impossible,
For those defects I have before rehears'd,
That ever Katherina will be woo'd.
125

Therefore this order hath Baptista ta'en,
That none shall have access unto Bianca
Till Katherine the curst have got a husband.

Grumio   Katherine the curst!
A title for a maid of all titles the worst.
130

Hortensio   Now shall my friend Petruchio do me grace,
And offer me disguis'd in sober robes
To old Baptista as a schoolmaster
Well seen in music, to instruct Bianca,
That so I may by this device at least
135

Have leave and leisure to make love to her,
And unsuspected court her by herself.

Enter **Gremio**, *and* **Lucentio** *disguised* [*as a schoolmaster*].

Grumio   Here's no knavery! See, to beguile the old
folks, how the young folks lay their heads together!
Master, master, look about you! Who goes there? ha!

Hortensio   Peace, Grumio, it is the rival of my love.
Petruchio, stand by a while.
142

Grumio   A proper stripling, and an amorous!

[*They stand aside.*]

Hortensio   Wait, Petruchio, I must go with you, for Baptista has my treasure locked away in his house. He has hidden away the jewel I prize most, his younger daughter, the beautiful Bianca, and refuses to allow me or any of her other suitors, my rivals for her love, to see her because he believes it impossible that Katherina will ever have someone woo her due to the flaws I have already told you about. Therefore, Baptista has given orders that no one shall be allowed to court Bianca until "Katherina, the Shrew" has a husband.

Grumio   "Katherina, the Shrew"! That's the worst name you can call a young woman!

Hortensio   Now, Petruchio, you may do me a favor. Present me to old Baptista. I will disguise myself in plain garments as a schoolmaster, expert in music, to instruct Bianca. By this stratagem, I will be able to have plenty of time to woo her and, unsuspected by her father, be alone with her to court her.

Grumio   This isn't wrongdoing. Look how the young folks plot together in order to fool the old folks.

[**Gremio** *enters with* **Lucentio**, *who is in disguise and carrying books.*]

Master, master, look! Who are these two?

Hortensio   Quiet, Grumio! It's a rival for my beloved. Petruchio, let's stand off to the side for a moment. [*He refers to* **Gremio**, *not realizing that the disguised* **Lucentio** *is the greater rival.*]

Grumio   [*to himself, speaking sarcastically of* **Gremio**] Such a handsome and romantic young lad!

[*They stand to the side to watch.*]

Gremio   O, very well, I have perus'd the note.
145   Hark you, sir, I'll have them very fairly bound—
All books of love, see that at any hand—
And see you read no other lectures to her.
You understand me. Over and beside
Signior Baptista's liberality,
I'll mend it with a largess. Take your paper too,
151   And let me have them very well perfum'd;
For she is sweeter than perfume itself
To whom they go to. What will you read to her?

Lucentio   What e'er I read to her, I'll plead for you
155   As for my patron, stand you so assur'd,
As firmly as yourself were still in place.
Yea, and perhaps with more successful words
Than you—unless you were a scholar, sir.

Gremio   O this learning, what a thing it is!

160   **Grumio**   O this woodcock, what an ass it is!

Petruchio   Peace, sirrah!

Hortensio   Grumio, mum! [*Coming forward.*] God save
you, Signior Gremio.

Gremio   And you are well met, Signior Hortensio.
Trow you whither I am going? To Baptista Minola.
165   I promis'd to inquire carefully
About a schoolmaster for the fair Bianca,
And by good fortune I have lighted well
On this young man; for learning and behavior
Fit for her turn, well read in poetry
170   And other books, good ones, I warrant ye.

Gremio   Oh, all right, I have read over the list of books for
   Bianca to study. Now listen to me, sir. I want them to be
   handsomely bound. They should all be books of love; make
   sure of that at least. And be sure that you read no other
   books to her. Do you understand me? Over and above
   Signior Baptista's generous payment, I will add my own
   liberal bonus. Also, take your list and have the books perfumed, for she to whom the books are to be given is
   sweeter than perfume itself. What do you plan to read
   to her?

Lucentio   [*speaking as if he is* **Cambio**] Let me assure you
   that whatever I read to her, I will plead for you as stead-
   fastly as if you were there to plead for yourself. Yes, and
   perhaps with even more success than you, unless you were
   a scholar, sir.

Gremio   Oh, what a wonderful thing this learning is!

Grumio   [*sarcastically*] Oh, what an unbelievable ass this
   fool is!

Petruchio   [*stifling his laughter at* **Grumio's** *remark*] Hush,
   man!

Hortensio   [*whispering to* **Grumio**] Grumio, be silent!

   [*speaking with elaborate but false politeness to* **Gremio**]
   Good day to you, Signior Gremio.

Gremio   [*with equally false politeness*] I'm happy to see
   you, Signior Hortensio. Do you know where I'm going? To
   Baptista Minola. I promised to search out a tutor for the
   lovely Bianca, and fortunately I have found this well-edu-
   cated and well-behaved young man, fully qualified to
   instruct her, well read in poetry and other books, good
   ones, I assure you.

Hortensio   'Tis well; and I have met a gentleman
   Hath promis'd me to help [me] to another,
   A fine musician to instruct our mistress;
   So shall I no whit be behind in duty
175   To fair Bianca, so beloved of me.

Gremio   Beloved of me, and that my deeds shall prove.

Grumio   And that his bags shall prove.

Hortensio   Gremio, 'tis now no time to vent our love;
   Listen to me, and if you speak me fair,
180   I'll tell you news indifferent good for either.
   Here is a gentleman whom by chance I met,
   Upon agreement from us to his liking,
   Will undertake to woo curst Katherine,
   Yea, and to marry her, if her dowry please.

185 **Gremio**   So said, so done, is well.
   Hortensio, have you told him all her faults?

Petruchio   I know she is an irksome brawling scold.
   If that be all, masters, I hear no harm.

Gremio   No, say'st me so, friend? What countryman?

190 **Petruchio**   Born in Verona, old [Antonio's] son.
   My father dead, my fortune lives for me,
   And I do hope good days and long to see.

Gremio   O sir, such a life, with such a wife, were strange;
   But if you have a stomach, to't a' God's name;
195   You shall have me assisting you in all.
   But will you woo this wild-cat?

Petruchio   Will I live?

Hortensio   [*with false enthusiasm*] How nice. And I have met a gentleman who has promised to help me to find another tutor, an excellent musician, to instruct our young lady, so I shall not fall the least bit behind you in serving the beautiful Bianca, whom I love so.

Gremio   [*competitively*] Whom *I* love so, and my deeds will prove it to be so.

Grumio   [*under his breath*] And his money bags will prove it to be so.

Hortensio   Gremio, this is no time to argue about our love. Listen to me, and if you speak to me politely, I'll tell you news that's equally good for both of us. If we can come up with an offer that is to his liking, this gentleman here [*indicating* **Petruchio**] whom I happened to meet, will try to woo quarrelsome Katherina, yes, and even marry her if her dowry is sufficient.

Gremio   [*skeptically*] If he does as he says, that would be good. [*lowering his voice so that only* **Hortensio** *can hear*] Hortensio, have you told him all her faults?

Petruchio   I know that she is an annoying, fighting shrew. If that's all that's wrong with her, gentlemen, I'm not worried.

Gremio   No, really, friend? What country are you from?

Petruchio   Born in Verona. I am old Antonio's son. My father has died, but my fortune is alive and well, and I hope to have many good years ahead of me.

Gremio   Sir, such a life with such a wife would be very strange! But, if you have the guts, go right ahead, by God. You'll have me helping you in any way I can. But do you really intend to woo this wildcat?

Petruchio   As surely as I live.

Grumio   Will he woo her? ay—or I'll hang her.

Petruchio   Why came I hither but to that intent?
Think you a little din can daunt mine ears?
200   Have I not in my time heard lions roar?
Have I not heard the sea, puff'd up with winds,
Rage like an angry boar chafed with sweat?
Have I not heard great ordnance in the field,
And heaven's artillery thunder in the skies?
205   Have I not in a pitched battle heard
Loud 'larums, neighing steeds, and trumpets' clang?
And do you tell me of a woman's tongue,
That gives not half so great a blow to hear
As will a chestnut in a farmer's fire?
Tush, tush, fear boys with bugs.

Grumio   For he fears none.

211 **Gremio**   Hortensio, hark.
This gentleman is happily arriv'd,
My mind presumes, for his own good and [ours].

Hortensio   I promis'd we would be contributors,
215   And bear his charging of wooing, whatsoe'er.

Gremio   And so we will, provided that he win her.

Grumio   I would I were as sure of a good dinner.

Enter **Tranio** *brave,* [*as Lucentio,*] *and* **Biondello**.

Tranio   Gentlemen, God save you. If I may be bold,
Tell me, I beseech you, which is the readiest way
220   To the house of Signior Baptista Minola?

Biondello   He that has the two fair daughters? is't he
you mean?

Tranio   Even he, Biondello.

Grumio [*to himself*] Will he woo her? Yes, or I'll hang her.

Petruchio I came here for no other reason but to do so. Do you think a little racket can hurt my ears? Haven't I heard lions roar? Haven't I, in my day, heard the wind-tossed sea roar like an angry boar in a rage? Haven't I heard large cannons in the field of battle, as well as the thundering in the sky of heaven's storms? Haven't I, in the heat of battle, heard loud battle cries, neighing steeds, and trumpets' clamor? And do you mean to warn me about a woman's tongue, which doesn't make half the explosion of a chestnut that bursts when roasted in a farmer's fire? Nonsense! I'm as likely to be afraid of the bogeyman.

Grumio [*to himself*] For he's not afraid of anyone.

Gremio Hortensio, listen. I think that it's a good thing that this gentleman has arrived, both for his sake as well as for ours.

Hortensio I've promised him that we will cover whatever expenses he incurs while wooing Katherina.

Gremio Indeed we will, assuming that he succeeds with her.

Grumio [*to himself*] I wish I were as sure of a good dinner.

[**Tranio**, *dressed as a gentleman, enters, along with* **Biondello**.]

Tranio [*speaking with elaborate politeness to* **Petruchio**, **Hortensio**, *and* **Gremio**] Good day, gentlemen. If I might be so bold, tell me, I beg of you, what is the quickest way to the house of Signior Baptista Minola?

Biondello The gentleman who has two beautiful daughters? Is he the one you mean?

Tranio That's the one, Biondello.

Gremio   Hark you, sir, you mean not her to—

Tranio   Perhaps him and her, sir; what have you
224   to do?

Petruchio   Not her that chides, sir, at any hand, I pray.

Tranio   I love no chiders, sir. Biondello, let's away.

Lucentio   [*Aside.*] Well begun, Tranio.

Hortensio   Sir, a word ere you go.
Are you a suitor to the maid you talk of, yea or no?

Tranio   And if I be, sir, is it any offense?

Gremio   No; if without more words you will get you
230   hence.

Tranio   Why, sir, I pray, are not the streets as free
For me as for you?

Gremio   But so is not she.

Tranio   For what reason, I beseech you?

Gremio   For this reason, if you'll know,
234   That she's the choice love of Signior Gremio.

Hortensio   That she's the chosen of Signior Hortensio.

Tranio   Softly, my masters! If you be gentlemen,
Do me this right: hear me with patience.
Baptista is a noble gentleman,
To whom my father is not all unknown,
240   And were his daughter fairer than she is,
She may more suitors have, and me for one.
Fair Leda's daughter had a thousand wooers,
Then well one more may fair Bianca have;
And so she shall. Lucentio shall make one,
245   Though Paris came in hope to speed alone.

Gremio   Excuse me, sir, but you don't mean the daughter—

Tranio   [*haughtily*] Perhaps both the father and the daughter, sir. What's it to you?

Petruchio   Not the quarrelsome one, at any rate, I hope, sir.

Tranio   I don't love quarrelers, sir. Biondello, let us go.

Lucentio   [*whispering to* **Tranio**] A good start, Tranio.

Hortensio   One thing before you go, sir. Are you a suitor to
the young lady you speak of, yes or no?

Tranio   And if I am, sir, is that a problem?

Gremio   Not if you leave without saying anything else.

Tranio   [*offended at the obvious insult*] Why, sir, don't I have
as much right to be on the streets as you?

Gremio   But not as much right to Bianca.

Tranio   Why would that be, if I might ask?

Gremio   If you must know, it's because she is the beloved of
Signior Gremio.

Hortensio   [*stepping forward to promote his cause*]
Because she is the beloved of Signior Hortensio.

Tranio   Calm down, sirs! Do me a favor, gentlemen, and
listen to me. Baptista is a noble gentleman, one who is
somewhat acquainted with my father. As beautiful as his
daughter is, she may have many suitors, including myself,
for one. Helen of Troy, the daughter of lovely Leda, had a
thousand suitors. Then Bianca may certainly have one
more, and so she shall. I, Lucentio, shall be one even if
Paris were here hoping to have the wooing all to himself.
[*Helen of Troy, although married to King Menelaus, eloped
with the Trojan hero Paris, resulting in the Trojan War.*]

Gremio   What, this gentleman will out-talk us all.

Lucentio   Sir, give him head, I know he'll prove a jade.

Petruchio   Hortensio, to what end are all these words?

Hortensio   Sir, let me be so bold as ask you,
250   Did you yet ever see Baptista's daughter?

Tranio   No, sir, but hear I do that he hath two:
The one as famous for a scolding tongue,
As is the other for beauteous modesty.

Petruchio   Sir, sir, the first's for me, let her go by.

255 **Gremio**   Yea, leave that labor to great Hercules,
And let it be more than Alcides' twelve.

Petruchio   Sir, understand you this of me, in sooth:
The youngest daughter, whom you hearken for,
Her father keeps from all access of suitors,
260   And will not promise her to any man,
Until the elder sister first be wed.
The younger then is free, and not before.

Tranio   If it be so, sir, that you are the man
Must stead us all, and me amongst the rest;
265   And if you break the ice, and do this [feat],
Achieve the elder, set the younger free
For our access—whose hap shall be to have her
Will not so graceless be to be ingrate.

Gremio   My, this gentleman will outtalk all of us.

Lucentio   [*speaking as **Cambio***] Let him run, sir. I'm sure he'll turn out to be a horse that quickly tires out.

Petruchio   Hortensio, what is all this talk about?

Hortensio   [*to **Tranio***] Sir, permit me to ask you whether you have ever seen Baptista's daughter?

Tranio   No, sir, but I have heard that he has two, one as famous for her scolding tongue as the other is for her beauty and good behavior.

Petruchio   [*stepping forward to join the conversation*] Sir, sir, I will take the first one, so you may forget about her.

Gremio   Yes, leave that labor to the great Hercules. It's harder than the other twelve he performed combined. [*Hercules, according to mythology, was required to perform twelve nearly impossible tasks in order to regain his honor after having, in a fit of insanity, killed his wife and their three children. Alcides was another name for Hercules.*]

Petruchio   Sir, let me tell you the truth of the situation. Baptista refuses to allow any suitor access to the younger daughter, the one you have been asking about, and will not promise to give her to any man until the elder sister is married. The younger will not be free until then.

Tranio   [*still speaking as if he is **Lucentio***] If that is the case, sir, then you are the man who must help us all, including me, and if you break the ice and accomplish this task, winning the elder and setting the younger free to the rest of us, whoever is fortunate enough to win Bianca will not be so ill-mannered as to fail to show his gratitude.

Hortensio   Sir, you say well, and well you do conceive,
270   And since you do profess to be a suitor,
You must, as we do, gratify this gentleman,
To whom we all rest generally beholding.

Tranio   Sir, I shall not be slack; in sign whereof,
Please ye we may contrive this afternoon,
275   And quaff carouses to our mistress' health,
And do as adversaries do in law,
Strive mightily, but eat and drink as friends.

Grumio, Biondello
O excellent motion! Fellows, let's be gone.

Hortensio   The motion's good indeed, and be it so,
280   Petruchio, I shall be your *ben venuto*.

Exeunt.

Hortensio   [*to* **Tranio**] Sir, you make a good point and your thinking is correct. And since you declare yourself to be a suitor, you must, along with the rest of us, pay this gentleman to whom all the rest of us shall owe a debt of gratitude. [*The gentleman he refers to is* **Petruchio**.]

Tranio   Sir, I will not be stingy, and to show my good intentions, let's get together this afternoon to drink to Bianca's health. Like those who are adversaries in court, let's make every effort possible, but outside the courtroom let us treat one another as friends.

Grumio *and* **Biondello**   [*speaking in unison and punning on making a motion in court*] An excellent motion! Let's go, friends.

Hortensio   [*continuing the pun*] The motion is a good one indeed, and since it is, Petruchio, I'll pay your share of the bill.

[*They all leave in good spirits.*]

Act two

Scene 1

Enter **Katherina** *and* **Bianca**.

Bianca   Good sister, wrong me not, nor wrong yourself,
To make a bondmaid and a slave of me—
That I disdain; but for these other [gawds],
Unbind my hands, I'll pull them off myself,
5   Yea, all my raiment, to my petticoat,
Or what you will command me will I do,
So well I know my duty to my elders.

Katherina   Of all thy suitors here I charge [thee] tell
Whom thou lov'st best; see thou dissemble not.

10 **Bianca**   Believe me, sister, of all the men alive
I never yet beheld that special face
Which I could fancy more than any other.

Katherina   Minion, thou liest. Is't not Hortensio?

Bianca   If you affect him, sister, here I swear
15   I'll plead for you myself, but you shall have him.

Katherina   O then belike you fancy riches more:
You will have Gremio to keep you fair.

Bianca   Is it for him you do envy me so?
Nay then you jest, and now I well perceive
20   You have but jested with me all this while.
I prithee, sister Kate, untie my hands.

Act two

Scene 1

A room in **Baptista's** *house in Padua.*

[**Katherina** *and* **Bianca** *enter.* **Bianca's** *hands are tied.*]

Bianca   [*weeping*] Dear sister, don't harm me or your reputation by making an indentured servant and slave of me. I
hate this! As for these other pretty things [*she refers to her
clothing and jewelry*], untie my hands and I will take them
off myself, yes, all my clothing right down to my petticoat.
Or whatever else you order me to do, I will, because I know
my duty to my elders.

Katherina   [*furiously*] I order you to tell me which, of all
your suitors, you love the best. And make sure that you
don't lie.

Bianca   Believe me, sister, out of all men living, I have never
yet seen that one special face that I could love more than
any other.

Katherina   Slut, you're lying! Is it Hortensio?

Bianca   If you like him, sister, I swear to you that I will plead
to him for you myself so that you may have him.

Katherina   [*suspicious over* **Bianca's** *apparent generosity*]
Oh, then I suppose that you prefer to be rich, so you want
to have Gremio who will provide generously for you.

Bianca   Is he the one making you envy me so? No, but you
must be joking, and I now see that you have been teasing
me all along. I beg you, sister Kate, untie my hands.

Katherina   If that be jest, then all the rest was so.

Strikes her.

Enter **Baptista**.

Baptista   Why, how now, dame, whence grows this
    insolence?
Bianca, stand aside. Poor girl, she weeps.
25 Go ply thy needle, meddle not with her.
For shame, thou hilding of a devilish spirit,
Why dost thou wrong her that did ne'er wrong thee?
When did she cross thee with a bitter word?

Katherina   Her silence flouts me, and I'll be reveng'd.

Flies after **Bianca**.

30 **Baptista**   What, in my sight? Bianca, get thee in.

Exit [**Bianca**].

Katherina   What, will you not suffer me? Nay, now I see
She is your treasure, she must have a husband;
I must dance barefoot on her wedding-day,
And for your love to her lead apes in hell.
35 Talk not to me, I will go sit and weep,
Till I can find occasion of revenge.

[*Exit.*]

Katherina   If you think that's a joke, then all the rest was, too.

[**Katherina** *slaps* **Bianca. Baptista** *comes in as she does so.*]

Baptista   [*to* **Katherina**, *furiously*] What is this, miss? Where does this appalling behavior come from?

[*to* **Bianca**, *tenderly*] Bianca, come here.

[*to himself*] Poor girl! She's crying. [*He unties her and speaks gently to her once again.*] Go do some needlework.

[*to* **Katherina**] Leave her alone! Shame on you, you child of a demon! Why do you harm her when she has never harmed you? When did she so much as speak an angry word to you?

Katherina   Her silence mocks me, and I'll have my revenge.

[**Katherina** *lunges at* **Bianca**, *who hides behind* **Baptista**.]

Baptista   [*to* **Katherina**] What, will you attack her in my presence?

[*gently, to* **Bianca**] Bianca, go inside.

[**Bianca** *leaves.* **Baptista** *looks at* **Katherina** *in disgust.*]

Katherina   What, can't you tolerate me? No, I see now that she is your treasure; she must have a husband, and because of your love for her I must dance barefoot on her wedding day and lead apes in hell. Don't talk to me! I will go sit and weep until I can find a way to take revenge. [*Unmarried older sisters would dance barefoot at their younger sister's wedding in hopes of catching a husband, and unmarried women were believed to lead apes in hell.*]

[**Katherina** *leaves, weeping.*]

Baptista   Was ever gentleman thus griev'd as I?
But who comes here?

Enter **Gremio, Lucentio** *in the habit of a mean man,*
Petruchio *with* [**Hortensio** *as a musician, and*] **Tranio**
[*as* **Lucentio**] *with his boy* [**Biondello**] *bearing a lute
and books.*

39 **Gremio**   Good morrow, neighbor Baptista.

Baptista   Good morrow, neighbor Gremio. God save
you, gentlemen!

Petruchio   And you, good sir! Pray have you not a daughter
Call'd Katherina, fair and virtuous?

Baptista   I have a daughter, sir, call'd Katherina.

45 **Gremio**   You are too blunt, go to it orderly.

Petruchio   You wrong me, Signior Gremio, give me leave.
I am a gentleman of Verona, sir,
That hearing of her beauty and her wit,
Her affability and bashful modesty,
50 Her wondrous qualities and mild behavior,
Am bold to show myself a forward guest
Within your house, to make mine eye the witness
Of that report which I so oft have heard.
And for an entrance to my entertainment,
55 I do present you with a man of mine,

[*Presenting Hortensio.*]

Cunning in music and the mathematics,
To instruct her fully in those sciences,
Whereof I know she is not ignorant.
Accept of him, or else you do me wrong.
60 His name is Litio, born in Mantua.

Baptista   [*in exasperation*] Was any gentleman ever so
afflicted as I? [*He suddenly sees a crowd of people
approaching.*] But who are these people coming here?

[**Gremio, Lucentio** *(disguised, in the clothing of a poor
man),* **Petruchio** *with* **Hortensio** *(disguised as a musician),* **Tranio** *(disguised as* **Lucentio***), and* **Biondello***, carrying books and a lute, all descend upon* **Baptista***.*]

Gremio   Good day, neighbor Baptista.

Baptista   Good day, neighbor Gremio. Greetings, gentlemen!

Petruchio   And to you, good sir. Tell me, do you have a
beautiful and virtuous daughter named Katherina?

Baptista   [*hesitantly, confused by* **Petruchio's** *description
of* **Katherina**] I have a daughter, sir, named Katherina.

Gremio   [*to* **Petruchio**] You are too hasty. Go about the
business properly.

Petruchio   Don't underestimate me, Signior Gremio. Let me
proceed.

[*to* **Baptista***, who listens in growing amazement*] I am a
gentleman of Verona, sir, who, hearing of your daughter's
beauty and wit, her pleasant disposition and maidenly
shyness, her wonderful qualities and gentle behavior, have
taken it upon myself to present myself as an ardent guest
within your house so that I can see for myself whether the
report I've heard so often is true. And, as my admission
ticket, I present to you my servant. [*He gestures toward*
Hortensio*, who is disguised as a tutor.*] He is skilled in
music and mathematics, capable of instructing her thoroughly in those fields of knowledge, about which I'm sure
she already knows a great deal. Accept his services from
me, or else I will feel insulted. His name is Licio; he was
born in Mantua.

Baptista Y' are welcome, sir, and he, for your good sake.
But for my daughter Katherine, this I know,
She is not for your turn, the more my grief.

Petruchio I see you do not mean to part with her,
65   Or else you like not of my company.

Baptista Mistake me not, I speak but as I find.
Whence are you, sir? What may I call your name?

Petruchio Petruchio is my name, Antonio's son,
A man well known throughout all Italy.

70 **Baptista** I know him well; you are welcome for his sake.

Gremio Saving your tale, Petruchio, I pray
Let us that are poor petitioners speak too.
[Backare]! you are marvellous forward.

Petruchio O, pardon me, Signior Gremio, I would fain
be doing.

75 **Gremio** I doubt it not, sir; but you will curse your wooing.
[Neighbor], this is a gift very grateful, I am sure of
it. To express the like kindness, myself, that have
been more kindly beholding to you than any, freely
give unto [you] this young scholar

[*presenting* LUCENTIO],

80   that hath been long studying at Rheims, as
cunning in Greek, Latin, and other languages, as
the other in music and mathematics. His name is
Cambio; pray accept his service.

Baptista [*hesitantly, unsure what to make of what he has heard*] You are welcome here, sir, as is he for your sake. But, concerning my daughter Katherina, as much as I regret saying it, you don't want her.

Petruchio [*deliberately misunderstanding* **Baptista**] I see you don't want to let her go. Either that or you don't like me.

Baptista Don't mistake my meaning. I merely say what I know to be true. Where are you from, sir? What is your name?

Petruchio Petruchio is my name, son of Antonio, a man well known throughout Italy.

Baptista I know him well. You are welcome here for his sake.

Gremio Please forgive me for interrupting, Petruchio, but let us, poor supplicants that we are, speak too.

[*whispering indignantly to* **Petruchio**] Back off! You are too pushy.

Petruchio Forgive me, Signior Gremio; I'm in a hurry. [*The verb "doing" can also mean having intercourse.*]

Gremio [*testily, to* **Petruchio**] I don't doubt it, sir, but you're going to damage your wooing.

[*to* **Baptista**] Neighbor, Petruchio's gift is a good one, I'm sure. In order to show you a similar kindness, I, who have as much reason to be grateful to you as anyone, freely offer you this young scholar [*he presents* **Lucentio**, *who is disguised as* **Cambio**] who for years has been studying at the university in Rheims. He is as expert in Greek, Latin, and other languages as this other man is in music and mathematics. His name is Cambio. Please accept his services.

Baptista   A thousand thanks, Signior Gremio.
85   Welcome, good Cambio.

[*To* **Tranio**.]

But, gentle sir, methinks you walk like a stranger.
May I be so bold to know the cause of your coming?

Tranio   Pardon me, sir, the boldness is mine own,
That being a stranger in this city here,
90   Do make myself a suitor to your daughter,
Unto Bianca, fair and virtuous.
Nor is your firm resolve unknown to me,
In the preferment of the eldest sister.
This liberty is all that I request,
95   That, upon knowledge of my parentage,
I may have welcome 'mongst the rest that woo,
And free access and favor as the rest;
And toward the education of your daughters,
I here bestow a simple instrument,
100   And this small packet of Greek and Latin books.
If you accept them, then their worth is great.

Baptista   Lucentio is your name, of whence, I pray?

Tranio   Of Pisa, sir, son to Vincentio.

Baptista   A mighty man of Pisa; by report
105   I know him well. You are very welcome, sir.
Take you the lute, and you the set of books.
You shall go see your pupils presently.
Holla, within!

Enter a **Servant**.

106

Baptista [*bowing to* **Gremio**] I give you a thousand thanks, Signior Gremio.

[*to* **Lucentio**, *disguised as* **Cambio**] Welcome, good Cambio. [**Lucentio** bows to **Baptista**.]

[**Baptista** *bows in return before turning to address* **Tranio**.] But, dear sir, you appear to be a stranger. May I be so bold as to ask why you have come here?

Tranio [*masquerading as* **Lucentio**] I beg your pardon, sir, the boldness is mine in that, being a stranger in this city, I would like to be a suitor to your lovely and virtuous daughter Bianca. Nor am I unaware of your firm resolution concerning the marriage of the elder sister. This favor is all I ask that, after I have told you who my parents are, you will make me as welcome as the others who woo and let me have as much access and good will as the rest. And, for the education of your daughters, I present you this musical instrument and this small parcel of Greek and Latin books. Their value will be great if you will accept them.

Baptista Lucentio is your name? Where are you from, if I may ask?

Tranio From Pisa, sir. I am the son of Vincentio.

Baptista He is a powerful man in Pisa. I've heard a great deal about him. You are very welcome, sir.

[*speaking to* **Hortensio** *as* **Licio**] Take the lute,

[*speaking to* **Lucentio** *as* **Cambio**] and you take the set of books.

[*speaking to both disguised scholars*] You shall see your pupils soon.

[*calling to a* **Servant**] Hello, come out here!

[*A* **Servant** *enters.*]

107

Sirrah, lead these gentlemen
To my daughters, and tell them both,
110 These are their tutors. Bid them use them well.

[*Exit Servant, with Lucentio and Hortensio, Biondello following.*]

We will go walk a little in the orchard,
And then to dinner. You are passing welcome,
And so I pray you all to think yourselves.

Petruchio Signior Baptista, my business asketh haste,
115 And every day I cannot come to woo.
You knew my father well, and in him me,
Left soly heir to all his lands and goods,
Which I have bettered rather than decreas'd.
Then tell me, if I get your daughter's love,
120 What dowry shall I have with her to wife?

Baptista After my death, the one half of my lands,
And in possession twenty thousand crowns.

Petruchio And for that dowry, I'll assure her of
Her widowhood, be it that she survive me,
125 In all my lands and leases whatsoever.
Let specialties be therefore drawn between us,
That covenants may be kept on either hand.

Baptista Ay, when the special thing is well obtain'd,
That is, her love; for that is all in all.

Petruchio Why, that is nothing; for I tell you, father,
131 I am as peremptory as she proud-minded;
And where two raging fires meet together,
They do consume the thing that feeds their fury.
Though little fire grows great with little wind,
135 Yet extreme gusts will blow out fire and all,
So I to her, and so she yields to me,
For I am rough, and woo not like a babe.

You there, take these gentlemen to my daughters and tell them both that these men are their tutors. Tell them I said to be courteous to them.

[*The* **Servant** *leads* **Lucentio** *and* **Hortensio** *out, with* **Biondello** *following.*]

[*to* **Gremio**, **Tranio**, *and* **Petruchio**] We'll go stroll in the garden and then go in to have dinner. You are all very welcome here, and I ask you to make yourself at home.

Petruchio   Signior Baptista, I'm in a hurry to complete my business [*that is, of wooing* **Katherina**], and I can't come to woo every day. You knew my father well, and because of that you also know me, the sole heir to all his property and possessions, which I have added to rather than decreased. So, tell me, if I win your daughter's love, what dowry shall you give me when we marry?

Baptista   Twenty thousand gold coins now, and when I die, half my lands.

Petruchio   And, for that dowry, assuming she survives me, I guarantee that if she is widowed, she shall inherit all my lands and the income from any leases I hold. Therefore, let contracts be drawn up to ensure that these terms will be kept by both of us.

Baptista   [*grimly*] Yes, when the one special thing is actually won: her love, that is. That's all that counts.

Petruchio   Why, that's nothing! For I tell you, father, I am as decisive as she is proud, and when two raging fires come together, they consume the thing that feeds their rage. Although little fires flare higher with a little wind, strong gusts will blow out the fire entirely. So I shall be to her, and thus she shall give in to me. For I am rough and don't woo like a little boy.

Baptista   Well mayst thou woo, and happy be thy speed!
But be thou arm'd for some unhappy words.

Petruchio   Ay, to the proof, as mountains are for winds,
141 That [shake] not, though they blow perpetually.

Enter **Hortensio** [*as Litio*] *with his head broke.*

Baptista   How now, my friend, why dost thou look so pale?

Hortensio   For fear, I promise you, if I look pale.

Baptista   What, will my daughter prove a good musician?

145 **Hortensio**   I think she'll sooner prove a soldier,
Iron may hold with her, but never lutes.

Baptista   Why then thou canst not break her to the lute?

Hortensio   Why, no, for she hath broke the lute to me.
I did but tell her she mistook her frets,
150 And bow'd her hand to teach her fingering;
When, with a most impatient devilish spirit,
"Frets, call you these?" quoth she, "I'll fume with
    them."
And with that word she strook me on the head,
And through the instrument my pate made way,
155 And there I stood amazed for a while,
As on a pillory, looking through the lute,
While she did call me rascal fiddler
And twangling Jack, with twenty such vild terms,
As had she studied to misuse me so.

160 **Petruchio**   Now by the world, it is a lusty wench!
I love her ten times more than e'er I did.
O, how I long to have some chat with her!

Baptista   May your wooing go well, and may you have good success. But be prepared for some harsh words.

Petruchio   As proof, just look at the mountains that stand firm although the winds never cease to blow.

[**Hortensio**, as **Licio**, *enters with his head bleeding.*]

Baptista   [*to* **Hortensio**] What has happened, my friend! Why do you look so pale?

Hortensio   [*clutching his aching head*] If I look pale, I promise you that it's from fear.

Baptista   Tell me, will my daughter be a good musician?

Hortensio   I think she would be a better soldier. Iron might be able to withstand her, but lutes never will.

Baptista   So you can't break [*that is, train*] her to the lute?

Hortensio   [*He holds up his broken instrument.*] No, but she has broken the lute to me. I merely told her that she was using the wrong frets and bent her fingers to teach her the fingering, when, with an impatient and devilish spirit, she cried, "Do you call these frets? I'll fret you with them!" And, with that, she struck me on the head and bashed a hole in the instrument with my skull, and there I stood for a while as if I were in a pillory [*that is, as if he were locked in the stocks*], stunned, looking out through the lute while she called me a "rascal fiddler" and a "twanging scoundrel" and twenty similar insults as if she had studied to abuse me so.

Petruchio   [*rubbing his hands together in gleeful anticipation*] Now, by God, that's what I call a spirited girl. I love her ten times as much as I did before. I can't wait to really get to know her!

Baptista   Well, go with me and be not so discomfited.
　　　Proceed in practice with my younger daughter;
165　She's apt to learn, and thankful for good turns.
　　　Signior Petruchio, will you go with us,
　　　Or shall I send my daughter Kate to you?

Petruchio   I pray you do. I'll attend her here,

> *Exit* [*Baptista with Gremio, Tranio,*
> *and Hortensio*]. *Manet Petruchio.*

　　　And woo her with some spirit when she comes.
170　Say that she rail, why then I'll tell her plain
　　　She sings as sweetly as a nightingale;
　　　Say that she frown, I'll say she looks as clear
　　　As morning roses newly wash'd with dew;
　　　Say she be mute, and will not speak a word,
175　Then I'll commend her volubility,
　　　And say she uttereth piercing eloquence;
　　　If she do bid me pack, I'll give her thanks,
　　　As though she bid me stay by her a week;
　　　If she deny to wed, I'll crave the day
180　When I shall ask the banes, and when be married.
　　　But here she comes, and now, Petruchio, speak.

Enter **Katherina**.

　　　Good morrow, Kate, for that's your name, I hear.

Katherina   Well have you heard, but something hard
　　　of hearing:
184　They call me Katherine that do talk of me.

Baptista [*to* **Hortensio**] Well, come with me and don't let yourself be discouraged. Go teach my younger daughter; she's quick to learn, and appreciates being treated kindly.

[*to* **Petruchio**] Will you come with us or shall I send my daughter Kate to you?

Petruchio Please send her.

[*All leave except for* **Petruchio**.]

I'll wait for her here, and woo her heartily when she comes. If she should shout, I'll tell her that she sings as sweetly as a nightingale. If she should frown, I'll say she looks as bright as morning roses washed with dew. If she's silent and refuses to speak a word, I'll praise her talkativeness and say that she has great eloquence. If she orders me to go away, I'll thank her as if she had just asked me to stay a week. If she refuses my marriage proposal, I'll ask what day I shall order the public announcement of our marriage and when we shall be married. But here she comes. Now, Petruchio, speak to her.

[**Katherina** *enters.*]

Good day, Kate, for that's your name, I hear.

Katherina You've heard well, but you're somewhat hard of hearing. Those who speak of me call me Katherina.

Petruchio   You lie, in faith, for you are call'd plain Kate,
And bonny Kate and sometimes Kate the curst;
But Kate, the prettiest Kate in Christendom,
Kate of Kate-Hall, my super-dainty Kate,
For dainties are all Kates, and therefore, Kate,
190   Take this of me, Kate of my consolation—
Hearing thy mildness prais'd in every town,
Thy virtues spoke of, and thy beauty sounded,
Yet not so deeply as to thee belongs,
Myself am mov'd to woo thee for my wife.

Katherina   Mov'd! in good time! Let him that mov'd
195   you hither
Remove you hence. I knew you at the first
You were a moveable.

Petruchio   Why, what's a moveable?

Katherina   A join'd-stool.

Petruchio   Thou hast hit it; come, sit on me.

Katherina   Asses are made to bear, and so are you.

Petruchio   Women are made to bear, and so are you.

201 **Katherina**   No such jade as you, if me you mean.

Petruchio   Alas, good Kate, I will not burden thee,
For knowing thee to be but young and light.

Petruchio   You are lying. You are called plain Kate, and lovely Kate, and sometimes Kate the curst, but you are Kate, the prettiest Kate in the world, Kate of Kate Hall, my precious Kate, for all Kates are precious. And, therefore, Kate, listen to me, my delightful Kate. Having heard your wonderful qualities praised everywhere I went and your beauty raved about—although the reports fall short of the beauty you possess—I had to come woo you and ask you to marry me.

Katherina   Oh, really? "Had to"! Let whoever made you come here immediately take you away. I knew as soon as I saw you that you "had to" be a piece of furniture. [*She means that he is not acting of his own free will.*]

Petruchio   What do you mean, a piece of furniture?

Katherina   A wooden stool. [*Calling someone a "join'd stool" was a common insult, meaning that the person was extremely stupid.*]

Petruchio   [*sitting down and pulling **Katherina** onto his lap*] You've guessed it! Come sit on me.

Katherina   [*struggling to get away from him*] Asses are made to bear burdens, and you're an ass!

Petruchio   [*refusing to let her go as she continues to struggle*] Women are made to bear children, and you're a woman.

Katherina   Well, I won't bear you, if you have me in mind. [*"Bear" here refers to sexual intercourse.*]

Petruchio   Now, good Kate, I wouldn't put too much weight on you, for, knowing that you are young and light— [*By "light" he means that she is a virgin.*]

Katherina   Too light for such a swain as you to catch,
205   And yet as heavy as my weight should be.

Petruchio   Should be! should—buzz!

Katherina   Well ta'en, and like a buzzard.

Petruchio   O slow-wing'd turtle, shall a buzzard take thee?

Katherina   Ay, for a turtle, as he takes a buzzard.

Petruchio   Come, come, you wasp, i' faith you are too
angry.

210   **Katherina**   If I be waspish, best beware my sting.

Petruchio   My remedy is then to pluck it out.

Katherina   Ay, if the fool could find it where it lies.

Petruchio   Who knows not where a wasp does wear his sting?
In his tail.

215   **Katherina**   In his tongue.

Petruchio   Whose tongue?

Katherina   Yours, if you talk of tales, and so farewell.

Petruchio   What, with my tongue in your tail? Nay,
come again,
Good Kate; I am a gentleman—

Katherina [*She finally manages to free herself from his hold and runs away from him. As they talk, he pursues her while she continues to run away from him.*] Too light of foot for such a clumsy oaf as you to catch, yet not weighing less than I should. [*She refers to the practice of clipping the edges off coins, making them lighter and therefore of less value.*]

Petruchio Should! Should buzz! [*He implies that rumors about immoral women buzz around like bees.*]

Katherina You've caught my meaning, like a buzzard. [*An insult referring to an untrainable hawk that catches the wrong prey.*]

Petruchio Oh, slow-flying turtledove! Shall a buzzard catch you?

Katherina Yes, mistaking me for a turtledove, which then catches the insect.

Petruchio Come, come, you wasp! I swear you are too angry.

Katherina If I am waspish, beware my sting.

Petruchio My cure, then, is to pluck it out.

Katherina Certainly, if you could find it, fool.

Petruchio Who doesn't know where a wasp has its sting? In his tail.

Katherina [*triumphantly, thinking she has outsmarted him*] In his tongue.

Petruchio Whose tongue?

Katherina Yours, if you talk of tails [*that is, genitalia*], and so, goodbye.

Petruchio What, with my tongue in your tail? No, come back, good Kate, I'm too much a gentleman.

117

| **Katherina** | That I'll try. |

She strikes him.

220 **Petruchio** I swear I'll cuff you, if you strike again.

Katherina So may you lose your arms.
If you strike me, you are no gentleman,
And if no gentleman, why then no arms.

Petruchio A herald, Kate? O, put me in thy books!

225 **Katherina** What is your crest? a coxcomb?

Petruchio A combless cock, so Kate will be my hen.

Katherina No cock of mine, you crow too like a craven.

Petruchio Nay, come, Kate, come; you must not look
so sour.

Katherina It is my fashion when I see a crab.

Petruchio Why, here's no crab, and therefore look not
230 sour.

Katherina There is, there is.

Petruchio Then show it me.

Katherina Had I a glass, I would.

Katherina   We'll just see about that.

[*She slaps him.*]

Petruchio   [*threateningly*] I swear I'll hit you if you slap me again.

Katherina   [*defiantly*] If you do, you will lose your arms. If you hit me, you are no gentleman, and if not a gentleman, then no arms. [*She is saying that if he were to hit her he would lose his coat of arms and thus he would no longer be a gentleman.*]

Petruchio   [*resuming his bantering tone*] Are you a herald, Kate? Oh, put me in your good books. [*A herald kept the list of those with the official status of gentleman.* **Petruchio** *means that he wants to be in favor with her.*]

Katherina   What is your crest? A coxcomb? [*a fool's cap, shaped like a cock's comb*]

Petruchio   A cock without a comb, if Kate will be my hen. [*A cock with its comb removed was one that was not aggressive.*]

Katherina   You'll not be my cock. You crow like one that will not fight.

Petruchio   No, come, come, Kate. You mustn't look so sour.

Katherina   It's how I look when I see a crabapple. [*that is, an irritable person*]

Petruchio   Why, there's no crabapple here, so don't look so sour.

Katherina   Oh, yes, there is.

Petruchio   Then show it to me.

Katherina   If I had a mirror, I would.

Petruchio What, you mean my face?

235 **Katherina** Well aim'd of such a young one.

Petruchio Now, by Saint George, I am too young for you.

Katherina Yet you are wither'd.

Petruchio 'Tis with cares.

Katherina I care not.

240 **Petruchio** Nay, hear you, Kate. In sooth you scape not so.

Katherina I chafe you if I tarry. Let me go.

Petruchio No, not a whit, I find you passing gentle:
'Twas told me you were rough and coy and sullen,
244 And now I find report a very liar;
For thou are pleasant, gamesome, passing courteous,
But slow in speech, yet sweet as spring-time flowers.
Thou canst not frown, thou canst not look askaunce,
Nor bite the lip, as angry wenches will,
Nor hast thou pleasure to be cross in talk;
250 But thou with mildness entertain'st thy wooers,
With gentle conference, soft, and affable.
Why does the world report that Kate doth limp?
O sland'rous world! Kate like the hazel-twig
Is straight and slender, and as brown in hue
255 As hazel-nuts, and sweeter than the kernels.
O, let me see thee walk. Thou dost not halt.

Katherina Go, fool, and whom thou keep'st command.

Petruchio   What, do you mean my face?

Katherina   [*sarcastically*] The little boy has hit the target.

Petruchio   By St. George, then I'm too young for you. [*St. George was an English soldier/hero, who was said to have killed a dragon.*]

Katherina   Yet you're wrinkled with age.

Petruchio   It's from worry.

Katherina   It doesn't worry me.

[**Petruchio** *recaptures* **Katherina** *as she starts to leave.*]

Petruchio   No, listen, Kate; I'm not letting you escape.

Katherina   I'll bother you if I stay. [*"Chafe" could mean either "irritate" or "excite."*] Let me go.

Petruchio   Not at all. To me, you seem quite gentle. I was told that you are rough and scornful and sullen, and yet I find that the rumors lie. You are pleasant, playful, more than courteous, slow to speak, yet as sweetly spoken as the fragrance of springtime flowers. You aren't even capable of frowning or looking suspiciously at others or biting your lip as females do when they are angry. Nor do you enjoy being quarrelsome, but you engage in gentle conversation, soft and pleasant to hear, with your suitors. Why does the world report that Kate has a limp? Oh, what a liar the world is! Kate is as straight and slender as the hazel-twig, with hair as brown as hazel nuts and sweeter than the hazel nut's kernel.

[**Petruchio** *releases* **Katherina**.]

Please, let me watch you walk; you don't limp.

Katherina   Go away, fool, and give orders to those you employ.

Petruchio   Did ever Dian so become a grove
As Kate this chamber with her princely gait?
260   O, be thou Dian, and let her be Kate,
And then let Kate be chaste, and Dian sportful!

Katherina   Where did you study all this goodly speech?

Petruchio   It is extempore, from my mother-wit.

Katherina   A witty mother! witless else her son.

265   **Petruchio**   Am I not wise?

Katherina   Yes, keep you warm.

Petruchio   Marry, so I mean, sweet Katharina, in thy bed;
And therefore setting all this chat aside,
Thus in plain terms: your father hath consented
That you shall be my wife; your dowry 'greed on;
271   And will you, nill you, I will marry you.
Now, Kate, I am a husband for your turn,
For by this light whereby I see thy beauty,
Thy beauty that doth make me like thee well,
275   Thou must be married to no man but me;
For I am he am born to tame you, Kate,
And bring you from a wild Kate to a Kate
Conformable as other household Kates.

Enter **Baptista, Gremio, Tranio** [*as Lucentio*].

Here comes your father. Never make denial;
280   I must and will have Katherine to my wife.

Baptista   Now, Signior Petruchio, how speed you with
my daughter?

Petruchio   Did Diana ever grace a woodland grove as well as Kate graces this room with her regal walk? Oh, you must be Diana, and she must be Kate. Then Kate may remain a virgin, and Diana may be amorous. [*Diana was the Roman goddess of hunting, associated with woodlands.*]

Katherina   [*sarcastically*] Where did you learn to say all these clever things?

Petruchio   It's off the top of my head, from my mother-wit [*that is, his natural intelligence*].

Katherina   Your mother must have been very witty, or else you would have ended up with no brains at all.

Petruchio   Am I not intelligent?

Katherina   Just enough to keep yourself warm. [*"He is wise enough who can keep himself warm" was a proverb meaning that one was very stupid.*]

Petruchio   Indeed, so I mean to do, sweet Katherina, in your bed. So let's stop all this chatting. To put it plainly, your father has given his consent that you should become my wife, your dowry has been agreed upon, and whether you agree or not, I am going to marry you. Now, Kate, I am the right husband for you, for I swear by the sun by which I see your beauty—that beauty that makes me like you very well—you must marry no one but me, for I am the man born to tame you, Kate, and change you from a wild Kate to a Kate as obedient as other domesticated Kates. [**Petruchio** *is equating* "**Kate**" *to* "*cat.*"]

Here comes your father. Don't deny it. I must and will have Katherina for my wife.

[**Baptista**, **Gremio**, *and* **Tranio** *enter.*]

Baptista   [*hesitantly*] Now, Signior Petruchio, what progress are you making with my daughter?

Petruchio   How but well, sir? how but well?
It were impossible I should speed amiss.

Baptista   Why, how now, daughter Katherine, in your
284   dumps?

Katherina   Call you me daughter? Now I promise you
You have show'd a tender fatherly regard,
To wish me wed to one half lunatic,
A madcap ruffian and a swearing Jack,
That thinks with oaths to face the matter out.

Petruchio   Father, 'tis thus: yourself and all the world,
291   That talk'd of her, have talk'd amiss of her.
If she be curst, it is for policy,
For she's not froward, but modest as the dove;
She is not hot, but temperate as the morn;
295   For patience she will prove a second Grissel,
And Roman Lucrece for her chastity;
And to conclude, we have 'greed so well together
That upon Sunday is the wedding-day.

Katherina   I'll see thee hang'd on Sunday first.

Gremio   Hark, Petruchio, she says she'll see thee
300   hang'd first.

Tranio   Is this your speeding? Nay then good night our part!

Petruchio   Very well, of course, sir, very well. It wasn't possible that I should fail.

Baptista   [*with false heartiness*] Why, how are you, daughter Katherina? Down in the dumps?

Katherina   Do you dare to call me "daughter"? You have shown quite the tender fatherly love, to wish me to marry someone who is one-half madman, one-half reckless brute and a cursing fool who thinks that all he has to do is swear in order to bluff his way through.

Petruchio   [*to* **Baptista**] Father, this is how it is—you and all the world that have spoken of her have lied. If she is difficult, it's just an act. She isn't uncooperative, but as gentle as the dove. She isn't hot tempered, but as mild as the morning. She is as patient as if she were a second Griselda, and as pure as the Roman Lucretia. And, to conclude the matter, we have gotten along so well that the wedding is to be on Sunday. [*Griselda was a wife famed for her submissiveness. Lucretia was a woman who so valued her sexual chastity that, because she was raped, she committed suicide.*]

Katherina   [*furiously*] I'll see you hanged on Sunday first!

Gremio   Do you hear, Petruchio? She says she'll see you hanged first.

Tranio   [*speaking as* **Lucentio**] This is what you call doing "well"? Well, then, so much for our plans.

Petruchio   Be patient, gentlemen, I choose her for myself.
If she and I be pleas'd, what's that to you?
'Tis bargain'd 'twixt us twain, being alone,
305   That she shall still be curst in company.
I tell you, 'tis incredible to believe
How much she loves me. O, the kindest Kate,
She hung about my neck, and kiss on kiss
She vied so fast, protesting oath on oath,
310   That in a twink she won me to her love.
O, you are novices! 'tis a world to see
How tame, when men and women are alone,
A meacock wretch can make the curstest shrew.
Give me thy hand, Kate, I will unto Venice
315   To buy apparel 'gainst the wedding-day.
Provide the feast, father, and bid the guests,
I will be sure my Katherine shall be fine.

Baptista   I know not what to say, but give me your hands.
God send you joy, Petruchio, 'tis a match.

Gremio, Tranio   Amen, say we. We will be witnesses.

321   **Petruchio**   Father, and wife, and gentlemen, adieu.
I will to Venice, Sunday comes apace.
We will have rings and things, and fine array;
And kiss me, Kate, we will be married a' Sunday.

Exeunt Petruchio and Katherine [severally].

325   **Gremio**   Was ever match clapp'd up so suddenly?

Baptista   Faith, gentlemen, now I play a merchant's part,
And venture madly on a desperate mart.

Tranio   'Twas a commodity lay fretting by you;
'Twill bring you gain, or perish on the seas.

330   **Baptista**   The gain I seek is, quiet [in] the match.

Petruchio   Calm down, gentlemen. I've chosen her for myself. If she and I are happy, what's it to you? We agreed when we were alone that when we are with others she shall still be shrewish. I assure you, it's hard to believe how much she loves me. Oh, she is the sweetest Kate! She hung on my neck and piled one kiss after another on me, vowing many loving vows, so that in a twinkling she had won me to her love. Oh, you are amateurs! It's amazing to see, when men and women are alone, how tame the meekest wretch of a man can make the worst shrew. Give me your hand, Kate. I will go to Venice to buy garments for the wedding day. Order the feast, father, and invite the guests. I want to be sure my Katherina shall be finely gowned.

Baptista   I don't know what to say. But let's shake hands. May God give you happiness, Petruchio! It's a match!

Gremio and **Tranio**   Amen to that! We will be witnesses.

Petruchio   Father, and wife, and gentlemen, goodbye. I'm off to Venice. Sunday will be here soon. We'll have rings and things and fine clothing. Kiss me, Kate, we're going to be married on Sunday.

[**Petruchio** and **Katherina** exit in separate directions, with **Katherina** glaring at him over her shoulder.]

Gremio   [in amazement] Was a marriage agreement ever slapped together so quickly?

Baptista   Indeed, gentlemen, I'm like a merchant engaged in a risky business venture in a dangerous market.

Tranio   You have a salable item that was going to waste. It will either bring you profit or be lost at sea.

Baptista   The only gain I seek is a peaceful marriage.

Gremio   No doubt but he hath got a quiet catch.
But now, Baptista, to your younger daughter;
Now is the day we long have looked for.
I am your neighbor, and was suitor first.

335 **Tranio**   And I am one that love Bianca more
Than words can witness, or your thoughts can guess.

Gremio   Youngling, thou canst not love so dear as I.

Tranio   Greybeard, thy love doth freeze.

Gremio   But thine doth fry.
Skipper, stand back, 'tis age that nourisheth.

Tranio   But youth in ladies' eyes that flourisheth.

Baptista   Content you, gentlemen, I will compound
341   this strife.
'Tis deeds must win the prize, and he of both
That can assure my daughter greatest dower
Shall have my Bianca's love.
345   Say, Signior Gremio, what can you assure her?

Gremio   [*ironically*] I'm sure that Petruchio has gotten a peaceful catch. But, now, Baptista, about your younger daughter. Today is the day we have all been waiting for. I am your neighbor and was her first suitor. [*He implies that because he was first, he has the greatest right to marry* **Bianca**.]

Tranio   [*speaking as* **Lucentio**] And I am the one who loves Bianca more than words can say or you can even imagine.

Gremio   Youngster, you can't love her as much as I do.

Tranio   Old man, your love is like ice.

Gremio   But yours is too hot. Stand back, lightweight. Mature lovers are tender and caring.

Tranio   [*triumphantly*] But when ladies see young men's good looks, youth is what they choose.

Baptista   Calm down, gentlemen; I will settle this quarrel. Actions will win the prize, and of the two of you, the one who can guarantee my daughter the biggest dowry will have my Bianca's love.

[*to* **Gremio** *only*] So, Signior Gremio, what can you promise her?

Gremio   First, as you know, my house within the city
Is richly furnished with plate and gold,
Basins and ewers to lave her dainty hands;
My hangings all of Tyrian tapestry;
350 In ivory coffers I have stuff'd my crowns;
In cypress chests my arras counterpoints,
Costly apparel, tents, and canopies,
Fine linen, Turkey cushions boss'd with pearl,
Valens of Venice gold in needle-work;
355 Pewter and brass, and all things that belongs
To house or house-keeping. Then at my farm
I have a hundred milch-kine to the pail,
Six score fat oxen standing in my stalls,
And all things answerable to this portion.
360 Myself am strook in years, I must confess,
And if I die to-morrow, this is hers,
If whilst I live she will be only mine.

Tranio   That "only" came well in. Sir, list to me:
I am my father's heir and only son.
365 If I may have your daughter to my wife,
I'll leave her houses three or four as good,
Within rich Pisa walls, as any one
Old Signior Gremio has in Padua,
Besides two thousand ducats by the year
370 Of fruitful land, all which shall be her jointer.
What, have I pinch'd you, Signior Gremio?

Gremio   Two thousand ducats by the year of land!
[*Aside.*] My land amounts not to so much in all.—
That she shall have, besides an argosy
375 That now is lying in Marsellis road.
What, have I chok'd you with an argosy?

Gremio   First, as you know, my house here in Padua is richly furnished with silver and gold utensils and dishes, and with basins and pitchers to wash her dainty hands. My wall hangings are all of Tyrian tapestry. I have ivory chests stuffed with gold coins and cypress chests filled with expensive bed covers from Arras, France. I also have costly garments, bed hangings, quilts, and canopies, fine linen, cushions made in Turkey and embroidered with pearls, a valance from Venice with gold embroidery, pewter and brass, and all other items needed in a household. Then, at my farm, I have the proceeds from the sale of the milk from one hundred cows, one hundred twenty fattened oxen in my stalls, and everything else appropriate to a dowry like this. I must admit that I am rather old, and if I should die tomorrow, all this becomes hers if she will be only mine while I live.

Tranio   [*speaking as* **Lucentio**] That word "only" is the crucial word.

[*to* **Baptista**] Listen to me, sir. I am my father's heir and *only* son. [*He stresses the word "only" to emphasize that he will not be dividing his inheritance with anyone else.*] If I may have your daughter as my wife, I'll leave her, in Pisa, three or four houses just as good as any house old Signior Gremio has in Padua, plus two thousand gold coins per year in income from fertile properties I rent out; all this shall be her marriage settlement.

[*in response to a strangled exclamation by* **Gremio**] What is it? Have I hurt you, Signior Gremio?

Gremio   Two thousand gold coins per year in rents!

[*to himself*] My land isn't worth nearly so much.

[*to* **Baptista**] She shall have all that I've offered, plus a merchant ship that is now anchored in Marseilles' harbor.

[*triumphantly, under his breath to* **Tranio**] What? Have I choked you with a merchant ship?

131

Tranio   Gremio, 'tis known my father hath no less
Than three great argosies, besides two galliasses
And twelve tight galleys. These I will assure her,
380   And twice as much, what e'er thou off'rest next.

Gremio   Nay, I have off'red all, I have no more,
And she can have no more than all I have;
If you like me, she shall have me and mine.

Tranio   Why then the maid is mine from all the world,
385   By your firm promise; Gremio is outvied.

Baptista   I must confess your offer is the best,
And let your father make her the assurance,
She is your own, else you must pardon me;
If you should die before him, where's her dower?

390 **Tranio**   That's but a cavil; he is old, I young.

Gremio   And may not young men die as well as old?

Baptista   Well, gentlemen,
I am thus resolv'd: on Sunday next you know
My daughter Katherine is to be married.
395   Now on the Sunday following shall Bianca
Be bride to you, if you make this assurance;
If not, to Signior Gremio.
And so I take my leave, and thank you both.

Exit.

Tranio   [*desperately increasing his offer*] Gremio, my father is known to have three large merchant ships, plus two big barges, and twelve galleys. I will promise her these as well as twice as much as any offer you make.

Gremio   [*defeated*] No, I've offered everything. I have nothing more, and she can't have more than all that I have.

[*to* **Baptista**] If you prefer me, she shall have me and my possessions.

Tranio   [*triumphantly*] Then I, of all men in the world, have won the girl according to your firm promise. Gremio is out-maneuvered.

Baptista   I must admit that your offer is the best, and assuming that your father confirms the promise, she is yours. However, if you will forgive me, if you should die before he does, what settlement will she receive?

Tranio   [*waving his hand dismissively*] That's a quibble. He is old; I'm young.

Gremio   [*snidely*] And don't young men die, as well as old ones?

Baptista   Well, gentlemen, I have decided the matter. As you know, my daughter Katherina is to be married next Sunday.

[*to* **Tranio**] Now, on the following Sunday, Bianca shall marry you, if your father backs up your promise. If not, Signior Gremio will have her. And so, I will go, and I thank you both.

Gremio   Adieu, good neighbor.
    Now I fear thee not.
400   Sirrah, young gamester, your father were a fool
    To give thee all, and in his waning age
    Set foot under thy table. Tut, a toy!
    An old Italian fox is not so kind, my boy.

Exit.

Tranio   A vengeance on your crafty withered hide!
405   Yet I have fac'd it with a card of ten.
    'Tis in my head to do my master good.
    I see no reason but suppos'd Lucentio
    Must get a father, call'd suppos'd Vincentio;
    And that's a wonder. Fathers commonly
410   Do get their children; but in this case of wooing,
    A child shall get a sire, if I fail not of my cunning.

Exit.

Gremio   Goodbye, good neighbor.

[**Baptista** *bows to* **Gremio** *and* **Tranio** *and then leaves*.]

Gremio   I'm not afraid of you any longer, young gambler.
Your father would be a fool to give you all that you've
offered and end up living out his life as a dependent upon
you. Ha! It's just your fantasy. Your father, an old Italian fox,
won't be so generous, my boy.

[**Gremio** *leaves, chuckling to himself.*]

Tranio   Damn your conniving, shriveled hide! I've bluffed
with only a ten in my hand.

I hope to help my master. I suppose that I, as the supposed
Lucentio, must get a father who will be the supposed Vincentio. Now, that's a riddle. Fathers usually beget children,
but in this case of wooing, a child shall beget a father, if I
don't fail in my plotting.

[*He leaves.*]

Act three

Scene 1

Enter **Lucentio** [*as Cambio*], **Hortensio** [*as Litio*], *and* **Bianca**.

Lucentio   Fiddler, forbear, you grow too forward, sir.
Have you so soon forgot the entertainment
Her sister Katherine welcom'd you withal?

Hortensio   But, wrangling pedant, this is
5   The patroness of heavenly harmony.
Then give me leave to have prerogative,
And when in music we have spent an hour,
Your lecture shall have leisure for as much.

Lucentio   Preposterous ass, that never read so far
10   To know the cause why music was ordain'd!
Was it not to refresh the mind of man
After his studies or his usual pain?
Then give me leave to read philosophy,
And while I pause, serve in your harmony.

15 **Hortensio**   Sirrah, I will not bear these braves of thine.

Bianca   Why, gentlemen, you do me double wrong
To strive for that which resteth in my choice.
I am no breeching scholar in the schools,
I'll not be tied to hours, nor 'pointed times,
20   But learn my lessons as I please myself.
And to cut off all strife, here sit we down:
Take you your instrument, play you the whiles,
His lecture will be done ere you have tun'd.

Act three

Scene 1

A room in **Baptista's** *house in Padua.*

[**Lucentio**, *disguised as* **Cambio**; **Hortensio**, *wearing a false beard, disguised as* **Licio**; *and* **Bianca** *enter.*]

Lucentio   [*speaking as* **Cambio**] Fiddler, control yourself. You're becoming too pushy, sir. Have you forgotten so soon the "entertainment" her sister Katherina gave you?

Hortensio   [*speaking as* **Licio**] But, quarrelsome scholar, Bianca is the goddess of heavenly harmony. So allow me to go first, and when we have spent an hour studying music, you shall have the same amount of time for your lecture.

Lucentio   [*dismissively*] Idiotic ass, you aren't educated enough to know why music was created. Wasn't it to refresh a person's mind after he has studied or to take his mind off his daily troubles? So let me go ahead and read philosophy with Bianca, and when I stop, you can refresh us with your harmony.

Hortensio   I won't put up with these insults, mister!

Bianca   Why, gentlemen, you both wrong me to argue over that which *I* have the right to decide. I am not a first-year student in a school, and I won't be controlled by schedules or timetables. I will study according to my preferences. So, stop all your arguing, and let's sit down here.

[*to* **Hortensio**] You take your instrument and play it for now. Cambio's lecture will be finished before you have even tuned your lute.

137

Hortensio   You'll leave his lecture when I am in tune?

Lucentio   That will be never, tune your instrument.

26 **Bianca**   Where left we last?

Lucentio   Here, madam:
  "Hic ibat Simois; hic est [Sigeia] tellus;
  Hic steterat Priami regia celsa senis."

30 **Bianca**   Conster them.

Lucentio   *"Hic ibat,"* as I told you before, *"Simois,"*
  I am Lucentio, *"hic est,"* son unto Vincentio of Pisa,
  "[Sigeia] tellus," disguis'd thus to get your love,
  "Hic steterat," and that Lucentio that comes-a-wooing,
35   *"Priami,"* is my man Tranio, *"regia,"* bearing
  my port, *"celsa senis,"* that we might beguile the old
  pantaloon.

Hortensio   Madam, my instrument's in tune.

Bianca   Let's hear. O fie, the treble jars.

40 **Lucentio**   Spit in the hole, man, and tune again.

Hortensio   So you will end his lesson when I'm in tune?

Lucentio   [*to himself*] That will never happen.

[*to* **Hortensio**] Tune your instrument.

Bianca   [*to* **"Cambio"**] Where did we stop?

Lucentio   Here, my lady. *Hic ibat Simois; hic est Sigeia tellus; Hic steterat Priami regia celsa senis.* [*Latin for "Here the Simois flowed; here is the Trojan plain; here stood old Priam's towering palace." He quotes from Ovid's "Letters from Heroines" (1.33–34).*]

Bianca   Translate the lines.

Lucentio   [**Lucentio**, *speaking as himself, lowers his voice whenever he speaks English.*] *Hic ibat,* as I told you before;

Simois, I am Lucentio;

hic est, son to Vincentio of Pisa;

Sigeia tellus; disguised this way to win your love;

Hic steterat, and the "Lucentio" who comes to court you;

Priami, is my servant Tranio;

Regia, pretending to be me;

celsa senis, so that we might trick the old fool Gremio.

Hortensio   [*still speaking as* **Licio**] My lady, my instrument is tuned.

Bianca   Let's hear it.

[**Hortensio** *plays his lute.*]

Oh, no! The high string is out of tune.

Lucentio   Spit on the tuning peg, man, and tune it again.

Bianca   Now let me see if I can conster it:
"*Hic ibat Simois*," I know you not, "*hic est* [*Sigeia*]
tellus," I trust you not, "*Hic steterat Priami*," take
heed he hear us not, "*regia*," presume not, "*celsa*
45   *senis*," despair not.

Hortensio   Madam, 'tis now in tune.

Lucentio   All but the base.

Hortensio   The base is right, 'tis the base knave that jars.
[*Aside.*] How fiery and forward our pedant is!
Now, for my life, the knave doth court my love:
50   Pedascule, I'll watch you better yet.

Bianca   In time I may believe, yet I mistrust.

Lucentio   Mistrust it not, for sure Aeacides
Was Ajax, call'd so from his grandfather.

Bianca   I must believe my master, else, I promise you,
55   I should be arguing still upon that doubt.
But let it rest. Now, Litio, to you:
Good master, take it not unkindly, pray,
That I have been thus pleasant with you both.

Bianca   [*loudly enough for* **Hortensio** *to overhear*] Now let me see if I can translate it.

[*like* **Lucentio,** *she lowers her voice when "translating."*] *Hic ibat Simois;* I don't know you;

hic est Sigeia tellus, I don't trust you;

Hic steterat Priami, be careful that Licio doesn't hear us;

regia, don't be over-confident;

[*Seeing how discouraged* **"Cambio"** *looks,* **Bianca** *suddenly offers him some encouragement.*]

celsa senis, don't lose heart.

Hortensio   [*bustling over*] My lady, it's tuned now.

Lucentio   All but the low string.

Hortensio   The low string is fine. It's the low fellow [*that is,* **Lucentio/Cambio**] who is out of tune.

[*to himself*] How hot-tempered and bold this scholar is! I swear the scoundrel is courting my love. Puny tutor, I'm keeping my eye on you.

Bianca   [*to* **Lucentio**] In time I may believe you, but I'm afraid to.

Lucentio   [*softly, to* **Bianca**] Don't be afraid,

[*more loudly for* **Hortensio/Licio** *to overhear, as if continuing the lesson*] for Aeacides was also called Ajax, named for his grandfather.

Bianca   I must take my instructor's word for it, or else, I assure you, I would still be arguing that issue with you. But let's drop the subject.

Hortensio   [*To Lucentio.*] You may go walk, and give
    me leave a while;
60   My lessons make no music in three parts.

Lucentio   Are you so formal, sir? Well, I must wait,
    [*Aside.*] And watch withal, for but I be deceiv'd,
    Our fine musician groweth amorous.

Hortensio   Madam, before you touch the instrument,
65   To learn the order of my fingering,
    I must begin with rudiments of art,
    To teach you gamouth in a briefer sort,
    More pleasant, pithy, and effectual,
    Than hath been taught by any of my trade;
70   And there it is in writing, fairly drawn.

Bianca   Why, I am past my gamouth long ago.

Hortensio   Yet read the gamouth of Hortensio.

Bianca   [*Reads*]
    "*Gamouth* I am, the ground of all accord:
    A re, to plead Hortensio's passion;
75   *B mi*, Bianca, take him for thy lord,
    C fa ut, that loves with all affection.
    D sol re, one cliff, two notes have I,
    E la mi, show pity, or I die."
    Call you this gamouth? Tut, I like it not.
80   Old fashions please me best; I am not so nice
    To [change] true rules for [odd] inventions.

Enter a **Messenger**.

[*to* **Hortensio/Licio**] Now, Licio, it's your turn. Good teachers, I hope that you won't be offended that I have been teasing both of you.

Hortensio   [*to* **Lucentio/Cambio**] You may take a walk and let me take over for a while. My music lessons don't require three parts.

Lucentio   [*as* **Cambio**] Are you so strict, sir? Well, I must wait [*to himself*] and keep an eye on you, for unless I miss my guess our fine musician, Licio, is becoming amorous.

Hortensio   [*as* **Licio**] My lady, before you touch the instrument, in order to learn the fingering, I must begin by explaining the fundamentals of the art of music. I must teach you the scales in a more pleasant, solid, and effective manner than anyone else of my profession can teach it. Here it is, written down neatly and elegantly.

Bianca   Why, I learned my scales years ago.

Hortensio   But read Hortensio's scales.

Bianca   [*reading aloud*] "I am the scale that is the basis of all harmony.

A re, to plead Hortensio's love;

B mi, Bianca, take for your husband;

C fa ut, the man who loves with all his heart;

D sol re, I have one key but only two notes;

E la mi, pity me or I will die."

[*to* **Hortensio/Licio**, *dismissively*] Do you call this a scale? Tsk! I don't like it. I prefer the old methods; I'm not so discontented as to exchange reliable methods for strange techniques.

[*A* **Servant** *enters.*]

Messenger   Mistress, your father prays you leave your books,
And help to dress your sister's chamber up.
You know to-morrow is the wedding-day.

85 **Bianca**   Farewell, sweet masters both, I must be gone.

[Exeunt Bianca and Messenger.]

Lucentio   Faith, mistress, then I have no cause to stay.

[Exit.]

Hortensio   But I have cause to pry into this pedant.
Methinks he looks as though he were in love;
Yet if thy thoughts, Bianca, be so humble
90   To cast thy wand'ring eyes on every stale,
Seize thee that list. If once I find thee ranging,
Hortensio will be quit with thee by changing.

Exit.

Servant   [*bowing formally to* **Bianca**] My lady, your father requests that you leave your studies to help decorate your sister's bedroom. You know that tomorrow is the wedding day.

Bianca   [*to both* **Hortensio/Licio** *and* **Lucentio/Cambio**] Goodbye, dear teachers. I must go.

[**Bianca** *and the* **Servant** *leave.*]

Lucentio   [*to the departing* **Bianca**] Then, my lady, I have no reason to stay.

[**Lucentio** *leaves.*]

Hortensio   [*to himself*] But I have good reason to find out more about this "scholar." He appears to me to be in love with Bianca.

[*to the now-absent* **Bianca**] Yet if you are so vulgar as to let your roaming eye be caught by any bit of bait, then go right ahead. If I find that you have wandered away from me, I will forget about you and find someone else.

[**Hortensio** *leaves.*]

Scene 2

Enter **Baptista**, **Gremio**, **Tranio** [*as Lucentio*], **Katherine**,
Bianca, [**Lucentio** *as Cambio*,] *and others, attendants.*

Baptista   [*To Tranio.*] Signior Lucentio, this is the
   'pointed day.
  That Katherine and Petruchio should be married,
  And yet we hear not of our son-in-law.
  What will be said? What mockery will it be,
5 To want the bridegroom when the priest attends
  To speak the ceremonial rites of marriage?
  What says Lucentio to this shame of ours?

Katherina   No shame but mine. I must forsooth be forc'd
  To give my hand oppos'd against my heart
10 Unto a mad-brain rudesby full of spleen,
  Who woo'd in haste, and means to wed at leisure.
  I told you, I, he was a frantic fool,
  Hiding his bitter jests in blunt behavior;
  And to be noted for a merry man,
15 He'll woo a thousand, 'point the day of marriage,
  Make friends, invite, and proclaim the banes,
  Yet never means to wed where he hath woo'd.
  Now must the world point at poor Katherine,
  And say, "Lo, there is mad Petruchio's wife,
20 If it would please him come and marry her!"

Tranio   Patience, good Katherine, and Baptista too.
  Upon my life, Petruchio means but well,
  Whatever fortune stays him from his word.
  Though he be blunt, I know him passing wise;
25 Though he be merry, yet withal he's honest.

Katherina   Would Katherine had never seen him though!

Exit weeping [*followed by Bianca and others*].

Scene 2

In front of Baptista's house in Padua.

[**Baptista**, **Gremio**, **Tranio**, **Katherina**, **Bianca**, **Lucentio**
enter, along with various guests and **Servants**.]

Baptista   [*to* **Tranio**, *still masquerading as* **Lucentio**]
Signior Lucentio, today is the day chosen for the wedding
of Katherina and Petruchio, yet we still haven't heard from
our son-in-law. What will people say? We'll look like fools if
we don't have a bridegroom when the priest begins to
perform the marriage ceremony! What do you have to say
about this shame of ours?

Katherina   [*with scathing bitterness*] The shame is no one's
but mine. I am forced to marry an insane, impulsive, ill-
mannered fellow whom I don't love, who wooed me hastily
but means to take his time about marrying me. I told you he
was a crazy fool, hiding his mockery behind down-to-earth
behavior. To earn himself the reputation of being a funny
man, he'll woo a thousand women, set the day for the marriage, order feasts, invite friends, and announce the marriage publicly, never having any intention to marry anyone
he has wooed. Now the whole world will point at poor
Katherina and say, "Look, there is crazy Petruchio's wife, if
he ever decides to come and marry her!"

Tranio   Be patient, dear Katherina and Baptista, also. I swear
to you that Petruchio's intentions are good, whatever mis-
fortune keeps him from keeping his word. Although he is
blunt, I know he has good judgment; although he likes to
joke, he is nonetheless honorable.

Katherina   I wish I had never met him!

[*She leaves, weeping bitterly, followed by* **Bianca** *and
others*]

Baptista   Go, girl, I cannot blame thee now to weep,
For such an injury would vex a very saint,
Much more a shrew of [thy] impatient humor.

Enter **Biondello**

Biondello   Master, master, news, [old news,] and such
31   news as you never heard of!

Baptista   Is it new and old too? how may that be?

Biondello   Why, is it not news to [hear] of Petruchio's
coming?

35 **Baptista**   Is he come?

Biondello   Why, no, sir.

Baptista   What then?

Biondello   He is coming.

Baptista   When will he be here?

Biondello   When he stands where I am, and sees you
41   there.

Tranio   But say, what to thine old news?

Baptista   [*to the departing* **Katherina**] Go, girl, I can't blame you for crying. Such an insult would anger a saint, much less a hot-tempered shrew like you.

[**Biondello** *enters.*]

Biondello   [*excitedly*] Master, master! I have news! Old news and news like you've never heard!

Baptista   It's new and old news, too? How can that be?

Biondello   Isn't it news to hear that Petruchio is coming?

Baptista   Is he here?

Biondello   Why, no, sir.

Baptista   What then?

Biondello   He's on his way.

Baptista   When will he be here?

Biondello   When he's standing where I am and looking at you there.

Tranio   But tell us, what is your old news?

Biondello   Why, Petruchio is coming in a new hat and
an old jerkin; a pair of old breeches thrice turn'd;
45   a pair of boots that have been candle-cases, one
buckled, another lac'd; an old rusty sword ta'en
out of the town armory, with a broken hilt, and
chapeless; with two broken points; his horse hipp'd,
with an old mothy saddle and stirrups of no kin-
50   dred; besides, possess'd with the glanders and
like to mose in the chine, troubled with the lampass,
infected with the fashions, full of windgalls, sped
with spavins, ray'd with yellows, past cure
of the fives, stark spoil'd with the staggers, be-
55   gnawn with the bots, [sway'd] in the back, and
shoulder-shotten, near-legg'd before, and with a
half- [cheek'd] bit and a head-stall of sheep's leather,
which being restrain'd to keep him from stumbling,
hath been often burst, and now repair'd with knots;
60   one girth six time piec'd and a woman's crupper
of velure, which hath two letters for her name fairly
set down in studs, and here and there piec'd with
packthread.

64 **Baptista**   Who comes with him?

Biondello   O, sir, his lackey, for all the world capari-
son'd like the horse; with a linen stock on one leg,
and a kersey boot-hose on the other, gart'red with
a red and blue list; an old hat, and the humor of
69   forty fancies prick'd in't for a feather: a monster,
a very monster in apparel, and not like a Christian
footboy or a gentleman's lackey.

Tranio   'Tis some odd humor pricks him to this fashion;
Yet oftentimes he goes but mean apparell'd.

Biondello   [*laughing uproariously*] Why, Petruchio is coming, wearing a new hat and an old jacket; an old pair of trousers so worn, he's had to turn them inside out; a mismatched pair of boots so old that they have been used to store candles—one of them has buckles, the other boot laces—a rusty old sword from the town arsenal with a broken hilt, no scabbard, and two broken garters. His horse is lame in the hips, it has a moth-eaten old saddle and stirrups that don't match, and besides that it has a swollen jaw, a runny nose, bad teeth, tumors all over, diseased ankles, a bad case of jaundice, swelling around the ears, a staggering disease; it's eaten up with parasites, has a sway-back, a dislocated shoulder, and knock-knees. The horse's bridle is hanging loose and the halter is made out of the cheapest leather, pulled so tightly to keep the horse from stumbling that it has broken again and again and now is tied in knots to repair it. The horse's girth strap has been mended six times, plus the saddle has a velvet strap from a lady's saddle with the lady's two initials beautifully lettered in metal studs, and here and there the whole thing is held together with twine.

Baptista   [*ignoring **Biondello's** description of **Petruchio** out of relief that he is coming*] Who is with him?

Biondello   Why, sir, his servant, as crazily outfitted as the horse is. He has a linen stocking on one leg and a cheap woolen stocking on the other, held up with a red and blue strip of cloth, wearing an old hat with an outlandish ornament in place of a feather. He looks like a monstrosity, an absolute monstrosity the way he's dressed, and not like a respectable servant or gentleman's valet.

Tranio   [*laughing at **Biondello's** description, yet mystified nonetheless*] Some odd mood must be spurring him on to look like this . . . although sometimes he does dress like a poor man.

151

Baptista   I am glad he's come, howsoe'er he comes.

75 **Biondello**   Why, sir, he comes not.

Baptista   Didst thou not say he comes?

Biondello   Who? that Petruchio came?

Baptista   Ay, that Petruchio came.

Biondello   No, sir, I say his horse comes, with him on
80   his back.

Baptista   Why, that's all one.

Biondello   Nay, by Saint Jamy,
I hold you a penny,
A horse and a man
85   Is more than one,
And yet not many.

Enter **Petruchio** *and* **Grumio**.

Petruchio   Come, where be these gallants? Who's at home?

Baptista   You are welcome, sir.

Petruchio   And yet I come not well.

Baptista   And yet you halt not.

Baptista   [*mopping his sweating brow*] I'm glad he has come, no matter how he looks.

Biondello   Why, sir, he isn't coming.

Baptista   Didn't you say he was coming?

Biondello   Who? That Petruchio was coming?

Baptista   [*in great frustration*] Yes, that Petruchio was coming!

Biondello   No, sir, I said that his horse was coming, with him on its back.

Baptista   [*impatiently*] It's all the same thing!

Biondello   [*quoting an old rhyme*]

No, by Saint Jamy,

I'll bet you a penny,

A horse and a man

Are two different things,

But not many.

[**Petruchio** *and* **Grumio** *arrive looking just as* **Biondello** *has described them.*]

Petruchio   [*heartily*] Say, where are all the guests? Who's here?

Baptista   [*with cold formality*] You are welcome here, sir.

Petruchio   Yet I don't feel "well come."

Baptista   [*taking* **Petruchio's** *words literally in order to avoid getting into an argument with him*] You don't have a problem with walking.

Tranio   Not so well apparell'd
90   As I wish you were.

Petruchio   Were it better, I should rush in thus:

[*Pretends great excitement.*]

But where is Kate? Where is my lovely bride?
How does my father?—Gentles, methinks you frown,
And wherefore gaze this goodly company,
95   As if they saw some wondrous monument,
Some comet or unusual prodigy?

Baptista   Why, sir, you know this is your wedding-day.
First were we sad, fearing you would not come,
Now sadder, that you come so unprovided.
100   Fie, doff this habit, shame to your estate,
An eye-sore to our solemn festival!

Tranio   And tell us, what occasion of import
Hath all so long detain'd you from your wife,
And sent you hither so unlike yourself?

Petruchio   Tedious it were to tell, and harsh to hear—
106   Sufficeth I am come to keep my word,
Though in some part enforced to digress,
Which at more leisure I will so excuse
As you shall well be satisfied with all.
110   But where is Kate? I stay too long from her.
The morning wears, 'tis time we were at church.

Tranio   See not your bride in these unreverent robes,
Go to my chamber, put on clothes of mine.

Petruchio   Not I, believe me, thus I'll visit her.

Tranio   [*speaking as* **Lucentio**] Nor are you as well dressed as I would like you to be.

Petruchio   Even if my clothing were better, I would still rush in this way. But where is Kate? Where is my lovely bride?

[*to* **Baptista**] How are you, father?

[*to the wedding guests*] Friends, I believe you are frowning. Why do you all stare as if you saw some strange omen, some comet in the sky or some frightening oddity? [*Comets were believed to be a warning that disaster was about to strike.*]

Baptista   [*with strong disapproval*] Why, sir, you know this is your wedding day! At first we were upset, fearing that you weren't coming, but now we're even more upset, seeing you arrive so badly dressed. Shame on you! Take off this outfit; it's a disgrace for someone of your social standing to wear, an eye-sore at our dignified ceremony!

Tranio   [*still as* **Lucentio**] And tell us, what major event has kept you from your wife for so long and sent you here looking so unlike yourself?

Petruchio   It would be boring to tell it and unpleasant for you to hear it. Let it be enough that I have come to keep my promise, although to some extent I will be forced to deviate from it, about which I will, when I have more time, explain my reasons to you later which will perfectly satisfy you.

But where is Kate? I've been apart from her for too long. The morning is speeding past. It's time we went to the church.

Tranio   Don't show yourself to your bride in these disgraceful clothes. Go to my place and put on some of my clothes.

Petruchio   No, indeed! I will see her dressed this way.

115 **Baptista**   But thus, I trust, you will not marry her.

Petruchio   Good sooth, even thus; therefore ha' done
    with words;
To me she's married, not unto my clothes.
Could I repair what she will wear in me,
As I can change these poor accoutrements,
120 'Twere well for Kate and better for myself.
But what a fool am I to chat with you,
When I should bid good morrow to my bride,
And seal the title with a lovely kiss!

Exit [with Grumio].

Tranio   He hath some meaning in his mad attire.
125 We will persuade him, be it possible,
To put on better ere he go to church.

Baptista   I'll after him, and see the event of this.

Exit [with Gremio and Attendants].

Tranio   But, sir, love concerneth us to add
Her father's liking, which to bring to pass,
130 As before imparted to your worship,
I am to get a man—what e'er he be,
It skills not much, we'll fit him to our turn—
And he shall be Vincentio of Pisa,
And make assurance here in Padua
135 Of greater sums than I have promised.
So shall you quietly enjoy your hope,
And marry sweet Bianca with consent.

Lucentio   Were it not that my fellow schoolmaster
Doth watch Bianca's steps so narrowly,
140 'Twere good methinks, to steal our marriage,
Which once perform'd, let all the world say no,
I'll keep mine own, despite of all the world.

156

Baptista But you surely won't marry her dressed like that.

Petruchio Of course, like this! So let's stop all the talking. She is marrying me, not my clothes. If I could fix those shortcomings in myself that she will have to put up with as easily as I can change these humble garments, it would be a good thing for Kate and even better for myself. But what a fool I am to be talking to you when I should be greeting my bride and sealing the bargain with a loving kiss!

[**Petruchio** *and* **Grumio** *leave.*]

Tranio [*speaking to those still remaining*] He must have some reason for his strange clothing. Let's try to persuade him, if possible, to put on something better before he goes to the church.

Baptista I'll go after him and see what happens.

[**Baptista, Gremio**, *and attendants leave.*]

Tranio [*softly, to* **Lucentio**] But, sir, in addition to Bianca's love we must also obtain the consent of her father. In order to do so, as I already mentioned to you, I must get a man— it's not really important what sort of man he is; we'll adapt him to our needs—and he shall become Vincentio of Pisa. He will make written guarantee in Padua of even greater sums of money than I have promised. And so, without any trouble in the process, you shall be able have your wish and marry sweet Bianca with her father's permission.

Lucentio If it weren't for the fact that my fellow schoolmaster watches every move Bianca makes so closely, I would consider eloping. Once our marriage has taken place, no matter who should object, I will keep her, no matter what the world says.

Tranio   That by degrees we mean to look into,
And watch our vantage in this business.
145 We'll overreach the greybeard, Gremio,
The narrow-prying father, Minola,
The quaint musician, amorous Litio,
All for my master's sake, Lucentio.

Enter **Gremio**.

Signior Gremio, came you from the church?

150 **Gremio**   As willingly as e'er I came from school.

Tranio   And is the bride and bridegroom coming home?

Gremio   A bridegroom say you? 'tis a groom indeed,
A grumbling groom, and that the girl shall find.

Tranio   Curster than she? why, 'tis impossible.

155 **Gremio**   Why, he's a devil, a devil, a very fiend.

Tranio   Why, she's a devil, a devil, the devil's dam.

Gremio   Tut, she's a lamb, a dove, a fool to him!
I'll tell you, Sir Lucentio: when the priest
Should ask, if Katherine should be his wife,
"Ay, by gogs-wouns," quoth he, and swore so loud,
161 That all-amaz'd the priest let fall the book,
And as he stoop'd again to take it up,
This mad-brain'd bridegroom took him such a cuff
That down fell priest and book, and book and priest.
165 "Now take them up," quoth he, "if any list."

Tranio   What said the wench when he rose again?

Tranio   We'll look into all that eventually and watch for our opportunity in this business. We'll get the better of the old man, Gremio; the busybody father, Minola; and the cunning musician, lover-boy Licio; all for the sake of my master, Lucentio.

[**Gremio** *returns.*]

[**Tranio,** *speaking as* **Lucentio,** *addresses* **Gremio.**]
Signior Gremio, are you back from the church?

Gremio   [*shaking his head in amazement*] With as much eagerness as I left school.

Tranio   Are the bride and bridegroom coming?

Gremio   Did you say "bridegroom"? He is more like a groom that cleans the stables, and a grumbling one besides, as that girl shall certainly find out.

Tranio   [*in amazement*] Is he even more disagreeable than she is? Why, that's impossible!

Gremio   He's a devil, a devil I say, a complete demon!

Tranio   Why, she's a devil, a devil I say, the mother of Satan!

Gremio   Tsk! She's a gentle lamb, a quiet dove, a pathetic pawn compared to him! Let me tell you about it, Signior Lucentio. When the priest asked if Katherina would be Petruchio's wife, Petruchio said, "Good God, yes!" and then he cursed so loudly that the priest dropped the prayer book, and as he stooped to pick it up again, that lunatic of a bridegroom hit him so hard that the priest and the book both fell to the floor. Then Petruchio said, "Now pick them up, if anyone dares."

Tranio   [*still in amazement*] What did Katherina say when the priest stood up again?

Gremio   Trembled and shook; for why, he stamp'd and swore
As if the vicar meant to cozen him.
But after many ceremonies done,
170   He calls for wine. "A health!" quoth he, as if
He had been aboard, carousing to his mates
After a storm, quaff'd off the muscadel
And threw the sops all in the sexton's face,
Having no other reason
175   But that his beard grew thin and hungerly,
And seem'd to ask him sops as he was drinking.
This done, he took the bride about the neck,
And kiss'd her lips with such a clamorous smack
That at the parting all the church did echo.
180   And I seeing this, came thence for very shame,
And after me I know the rout is coming.
Such a mad marriage never was before.
Hark, hark, I hear the minstrels play.

Music plays.

Enter **Petruchio, Kate, Bianca, Hortensio** [*as Litio*],
Baptista [**Grumio,** *and* **Train**].

Petruchio   Gentlemen and friends, I thank you for your pains.
185   I know you think to dine with me to-day,
And have prepar'd great store of wedding cheer,
But so it is, my haste doth call me hence,
And therefore here I mean to take my leave.

Baptista   Is't possible you will away to-night?

Gremio   She trembled and shook with fear because Petruchio stamped his feet and swore again as if he thought the priest meant to cheat him somehow. But, eventually, after all the rites were finished, he called out for wine. "To your health!" he shouted, as if he were on board a ship getting drunk with his fellow seamen after a storm. He drank up all the wine and threw the pieces of cake they put in the wine in the sexton's face for no other reason than that the man's beard was thin and straggly, and then he seemed to want the pieces back as he was drinking. When he was done, he grabbed the bride by the neck and planted such a loud smacking kiss on her lips that the church echoed with the sound. And I, having seen all this, walked out in disgust, and I know the rest of the guests are right behind me. There has never been such a mockery of a marriage. Listen! Listen! I hear the musicians.

[*Music can be heard as* **Petruchio**, **Katherina**, **Bianca**, **Baptista**, **Hortensio**, **Grumio**, *and other members of the wedding return.*]

Petruchio   [*loudly and jovially, speaking to those present*] Gentlemen and friends, I thank you all for making the effort to come. I know you think that you will dine with me today, and consequently have prepared a great wedding feast. However, I have urgent business that calls me away, and therefore I must now leave you.

Baptista   [*in disbelief*] Surely you don't intend to leave tonight?

190 **Petruchio**   I must away to-day, before night come.
Make it no wonder; if you knew my business,
You would entreat me rather go than stay.
And, honest company, I thank you all,
That have beheld me give away myself
195 To this most patient, sweet, and virtuous wife:
Dine with my father, drink a health to me,
For I must hence, and farewell to you all.

Tranio   Let us entreat you stay till after dinner.

Petruchio   It may not be.

Gremio   Let me entreat you.

Petruchio   It cannot be.

200 **Katherina**   Let me entreat you.

Petruchio   I am content.

Katherina   Are you content to stay?

Petruchio   I am content you shall entreat me stay,
But yet not stay, entreat me how you can.

Katherina   Now if you love me stay.

Petruchio   Grumio, my horse.

Grumio   Ay, sir, they be ready; the oats have eaten
206   the horses.

Katherina   Nay then,
Do what thou canst, I will not go to-day,
No, nor to-morrow—not till I please myself.
210   The door is open, sir, there lies your way;
You may be jogging whiles your boots are green.
For me, I'll not be gone till I please myself.
'Tis like you'll prove a jolly surly groom,
214   That take it on you at the first so roundly.

Petruchio I must leave today, even before night falls. Don't look so surprised. If you knew what my business is, you would beg me to leave rather than ask me to stay. Dear friends, I thank all of you who witnessed my giving myself away to this outstandingly patient, sweet, and virtuous wife. Dine with Baptista and drink a toast to my health, for I must leave. Goodbye to you all.

Tranio [*shocked at* **Petruchio's** *intentions*] Let us urge you not to leave until after dinner.

Petruchio It isn't possible.

Gremio [*also shocked at this serious breach of etiquette*] Let *me* urge you.

Petruchio It can't be done.

Katherina Let *me* ask you.

Petruchio I am content.

Katherina Do you mean that you're willing to stay?

Petruchio I'm content that you have asked me to stay, yet I can't stay, no matter how you ask me.

Katherina [*her temper rising*] Now, if you love me, stay.

Petruchio [*ignoring* **Katherina** *and addressing* **Grumio**] Grumio, get my horses.

Grumio They're all ready and stuffed full of oats.

Katherina [*her eyes flashing with anger*] Then do what you want, but I won't come with you today, or tomorrow for that matter, or until I feel like it! The door is open, sir, and nothing is stopping you. You may run along while your boots are new, but, as for me, I will not leave until I decide to do so. If you are so difficult at the very beginning of our marriage, you're likely to turn out to be an overbearing and ill-tempered husband. [*She tosses her head and turns her back to him.*]

Petruchio   O Kate, content thee, prithee be not angry.

Katherina   I will be angry; what hast thou to do?
   Father, be quiet, he shall stay my leisure.

Gremio   Ay, marry, sir, now it begins to work.

Katherina   Gentlemen, forward to the bridal dinner.
220   I see a woman may be made a fool,
      If she had not a spirit to resist.

Petruchio   They shall go forward, Kate, at thy command.
      Obey the bride, you that attend on her.
      Go to the feast, revel and domineer,
225   Carouse full measure to her maidenhead,
      Be mad and merry, or go hang yourselves;
      But for my bonny Kate, she must with me.
      Nay, look not big, nor stamp, nor stare, nor fret,
      I will be master of what is mine own.
230   She is my goods, my chattels, she is my house,
      My household stuff, my field, my barn,
      My horse, my ox, my ass, my any thing;
      And here she stands, touch her whoever dare,
      I'll bring mine action on the proudest he
235   That stops my way in Padua. Grumio,
      Draw forth thy weapon, we are beset with thieves;
      Rescue thy mistress if thou be a man.

Petruchio   [*speaking gently to her*] Oh, Kate, calm down and don't be angry.

Katherina   [*stamping her foot in rage*] I will be angry! What business is it of yours?

[*to* **Baptista** *who is trying to silence her*] Father, be quiet! He shall not leave until I'm ready to leave.

Gremio   [*chuckling in anticipation of the argument he expects to start between* **Katherina** *and* **Petruchio**] All right, sir, now here we go!

Katherina   [*loudly, to the wedding guests*] Gentlemen, let us go in to the wedding dinner. I see that a woman may be made to look like a fool if she doesn't have the guts to stand up for herself.

Petruchio   [*to* **Katherina**, *seeming to misunderstand her*] They shall go in, Kate, at your command.

[*to the guests*] Obey the bride, guests! Go to the feast; celebrate and drink heartily; get as drunk as you like to celebrate her virginity! Be rowdy and high-spirited, or, if not, you may drop dead. But as for my lovely Kate, she must come with me.

[*He then speaks as if addressing the guests, but in reality, he is talking to* **Katherina**.] No, don't look offended, or stamp your feet, or glare at me, or fume. I will be the master of whatever is mine. And she is my possession, my property; she is my house, my furniture, my field, my barn, my horse, my ox, my ass, my anything. And here she is, but don't dare to touch her! I'll fight against even the mightiest man if he tries to keep me from leaving Padua.

[*to* **Grumio**] Grumio, draw your sword! Thieves surround us! Rescue your mistress, if you're a man!

165

Fear not, sweet wench, they shall not touch thee, Kate!
I'll buckler thee against a million.

Exeunt Petruchio, Katherina, [and Grumio].

240 **Baptista**   Nay, let them go, a couple of quiet ones.

Gremio   Went they not quickly, I should die with laughing.

Tranio   Of all mad matches never was the like.

Lucentio   Mistress, what's your opinion of your sister?

Bianca   That being mad herself, she's madly mated.

245 **Gremio**   I warrant him, Petruchio is Kated.

Baptista   Neighbors and friends, though bride and
        bridegroom wants
    For to supply the places at the table,
    You know there wants no junkets at the feast.
    Lucentio, you shall supply the bridegroom's place,
250   And let Bianca take her sister's room.

Tranio   Shall sweet Bianca practise how to bride it?

Baptista   She shall, Lucentio. Come, gentlemen, let's go.

Exeunt.

[*to* **Katherina**] Don't be afraid, sweet lady! They shall not harm you, Kate! I'll defend you against a million!

[*Pulling a reluctant* **Katherina** *along,* **Petruchio** *and* **Grumio** *leave with swords drawn as if defending her from attackers.*]

Baptista [*seeing that some of the guests are going after* **Katherina**, **Petruchio**, *and* **Grumio**] No, let them go, "peaceful" people that they are.

Gremio [*laughing and mopping his eyes*] If they hadn't left soon, I would have died laughing!

Tranio [*shaking his head in wonderment*] There has never been a marriage so crazy as this one.

Lucentio [*speaking as* **Cambio** *to* **Bianca**, *who, like everyone else, is laughing*] My lady, what do you think of your sister?

Bianca [*laughing*] That she is insane herself, so this insane marriage should suit her.

Gremio I swear that Petruchio has met his match in her.

Baptista [*not knowing what else to do but to invite his guests to eat and drink at the banquet that has been prepared*] Neighbors and friends, although the bride and groom are not at their places at the table, you know that we have plenty of fine food for you at this feast.

[*to* **Tranio**, *as* **Lucentio**] Lucentio, you must sit in the bridegroom's place, and Bianca may take her sister's seat.

Tranio [*speaking as* **Lucentio**] Is sweet Bianca going to practice being a bride?

Baptista Yes, she is, Lucentio. Come, everyone, let's go.

[*Everyone leaves to celebrate the wedding of the now-absent bride and groom.*]

Act four

Scene 1

Enter **Grumio**.

Grumio   Fie, fie on all tir'd jades, on all mad masters,
and all foul ways! Was ever man so beaten?
Was ever man so ray'd? was ever man so weary?
I am sent before to make a fire, and they are com-
5   ing after to warm them. Now, were not I a
little pot and soon hot, my very lips might freeze
to my teeth, my tongue to the roof of my mouth,
my heart in my belly, ere I should come by a fire
to thaw me: But I with blowing the fire shall
10   warm myself; for considering the weather,
a taller man than I will take cold. Holla, ho,
Curtis!

Enter Curtis.

Curtis   Who is that calls so coldly?

Grumio   A piece of ice. If thou doubt it, thou mayst
slide from my shoulder to my heel with no greater
16   a run but my head and my neck. A fire, good
Curtis.

Curtis   Is my master and his wife coming, Grumio?

Grumio   O ay, Curtis, ay, and therefore fire, fire;
20   cast on no water.

Curtis   Is she so hot a shrew as she's reported?

Act four

Scene 1

Inside **Petruchio's** *house in the country.*

[**Grumio** *enters.*]

Grumio   Damn all tired, broken-down horses, damn all crazy masters, and damn the terrible roads! Was any man ever beaten as much as I am? Was any man ever as filthy? Was any man ever as tired? I've been sent ahead to make sure the fires are lit, and Petruchio and Katherina will be here soon to warm themselves. If I weren't like a little pot that is quickly heated up, my lips might freeze to my teeth, my tongue to the roof of my mouth, and my heart might freeze within my belly before I could find a fire to warm myself at. But, by blowing on the fire of my anger, I'll keep myself warm. In weather like this, a taller person than I would get sick. [*Proverbially, a small pot boils more quickly than a large one, and a short person gets angry faster than a tall one.*]

[**Curtis** *enters.*]

Curtis   Who is calling out like he's half-frozen?

Grumio   [*wearily*] A block of ice. If you don't believe me, you can slide all the way from my shoulders to my heels with only the length of my head and neck to give you a running start. Build the fire, Curtis.

Curtis   Are my master and his wife coming, Grumio?

Grumio   Oh, yes, Curtis, yes. And therefore build the fire, and don't throw any water on it.

Curtis   Is she as hot-tempered a shrew as they say?

Grumio She was, good Curtis, before this frost;
but thou know'st winter tames man, woman, and
beast; for it hath tam'd my old master and my new
25 mistress and myself, fellow Curtis.

Curtis Away, you three-inch fool! I am no beast.

Grumio Am I but three inches? Why, thy horn
is a foot, and so long am I at the least. But wilt thou
make a fire, or shall I complain on thee to our mis-
30 tress, whose hand (she being now at hand) thou
shalt soon feel, to thy cold comfort, for being slow
in thy hot office?

34 **Curtis** I prithee, good Grumio, tell me, how goes the world?

Grumio A cold world, Curtis, in every office but
thine, and therefore fire. Do thy duty and have thy
duty, for my master and mistress are almost frozen
to death.

Curtis There's fire ready, and therefore, good
40 Grumio, the news.

Grumio Why, "Jack, boy! ho, boy!" and as much
news as wilt thou.

Curtis Come, you are so full of cony-catching!

Grumio   She was before being out in this cold, good Curtis. But you know how winter can crush a man, a woman, or an animal, and it has crushed my old master, my new mistress, and me, my friend Curtis.

Curtis   [*deeply offended*] You three-inch-tall fool! I'm not an animal!

Grumio   [*indignantly*] I'm only three inches tall? Well, your cuckold's horn is a foot long, and I'm at least that tall. So make the fire, or I will report to our mistress about you, and, since she is now at hand, you shall soon be slapped with her hand. That will be a cold comfort to you for being so slow in your job of building the fire. [**Grumio's** *remark about the cuckold's horn is an insult. If a man's wife was unfaithful to him, the man (the cuckold) would be forced to wear horns on his head and would be marched through the streets for people to ridicule him.*]

Curtis   [*going to build the fire*] So, tell me, good Grumio, what's new in the world?

Grumio   It's a cold world, Curtis, for everyone but those who do the same kind of work you do. So build the fire. Do your duty if you want to keep your job, for my master and mistress are nearly frozen to death.

Curtis   There, the fire is ready. So now tell me the news, good Grumio.

Grumio   [*singing the first line of a popular song*] "Jack, boy! Ho! Boy!" and as much news as you want.

Curtis   Stop it! You're always joking around!

Grumio   Why, therefore fire, for I have caught
45   extreme cold. Where's the cook? Is supper
ready, the house trimm'd, rushes strew'd, cobwebs swept, the servingmen in their new fustian,
[their] white stockings, and every officer his wedding garment on? Be the Jacks fair within, the
Gills fair without, the carpets laid, and every thing
51   in order?

Curtis   All ready; and therefore I pray thee,
news.

Grumio   First, know my horse is tir'd, my master and
55   mistress fall'n out.

Curtis   How?

Grumio   Out of their saddles into the dirt, and
thereby hangs a tale.

Curtis   Let's ha't, good Grumio.

60 **Grumio**   Lend thine ear.

Curtis   Here.

Grumio   There.

[*Strikes him.*]

Curtis   This 'tis to feel a tale, not to hear a tale.

Grumio   And therefore 'tis call'd a sensible tale;
65   and this cuff was but to knock at your ear, and
beseech list'ning. Now I begin: *Imprimis*, we came
down a foul hill, my master riding behind my mistress—

Curtis   Both of one horse?

70 **Grumio**   What's that to thee?

Curtis   Why, a horse.

Grumio   Why, then, stoke the fire, for I'm frozen through. Where is the cook? Is supper ready? Is the house cleaned, the rushes spread on the floor, the cobwebs swept? Are the lower servants wearing their new uniforms and white stockings? Do all the upper servants have their wedding garments on? Are the glasses and cups clean, inside and out, the tablecloths on the table, and everything in proper order?

Curtis   It's all ready, so, please, tell me the news.

Grumio   First of all, my horse is tired, and my master and mistress have had a falling out. [*He seems to be saying that they are quarreling.*]

Curtis   Why?

Grumio   They've fallen out of their saddles into the mud, and that's quite a story.

Curtis   [*his eyes sparkling in anticipation*] Tell me, Grumio.

Grumio   Lend me your ear.

Curtis   [*Thinking* **Grumio** *is going to tell him a secret,* **Curtis** *leans forward.*] Here.

Grumio   There! [*He hits* **Curtis**.]

Curtis   [*rubbing his injured ear*] That's how to feel a story, not to hear it.

Grumio   That's why it's called a "sensible" story. I only hit you to knock on the "door" of your ear and make sure I had your attention. Now I'll begin. First, we came down a nasty hill, my master riding behind my mistress—

Curtis   Both on one horse?

Grumio   What is it to you?

Curtis   Why, it's the difference of one horse or two.

173

Grumio   Tell thou the tale. But hadst thou not
cross'd me, thou shouldst have heard how her horse
fell, and she under her horse; thou shouldst have
75   heard in how miry a place, how she was be-
moil'd, how he left her with the horse upon her,
how he beat me because her horse stumbled, how
she waded through the dirt to pluck him off me;
how he swore, how she pray'd, that never pray'd
80   before; how I cried, how the horses ran away,
how her bridle was burst; how I lost my crupper,
with many things of worthy memory, which now
shall die in oblivion, and thou return unexperienc'd
84   to thy grave.

Curtis   By this reck'ning he is more shrew than she.

Grumio   Ay, and that thou and the proudest of
you all shall find when he comes home. But what
talk I of this? Call forth Nathaniel, Joseph, Nicholas,
90   Philip, Walter, Sugarsop and the rest; let their
heads be slickly comb'd, their blue coats brush'd
and their garters of an indifferent knit; let them curtsy
with their left legs, and not presume to touch a hair
of my master's horse-tail till they kiss their hands.
95   Are they all ready?

Curtis   They are.

Grumio   Call them forth.

Curtis   Do you hear, ho? You must meet my master
to countenance my mistress.

100 **Grumio**   Why, she hath a face of her own.

Curtis   Who knows not that?

Grumio   Then *you* tell the story. If you hadn't made me angry, you would have heard that her horse fell right on top of her; that it was in a muddy place, that she got covered with dirt and muck, that he left her there with the horse on top of her, that he beat me because her horse stumbled, that she then waded through the mud to pull him off me, that he cursed, that she begged—she who had never begged before—that I hollered, that the horses ran away, that her bridle tore in two, that I lost one of the straps that hold my saddle in place, along with many other memorable stories, which will all go untold and you shall go to your grave in ignorance.

Curtis   From what you say, it sounds like he's more a shrew than she is!

Grumio   Yes, which you as well as the snootiest servant here shall discover when he comes home. But why am I telling you this? Call Nathaniel, Joseph, Nicholas, Philip, Walter, Sugarsop, and the rest of the servants. Make sure that their hair is neatly combed, their blue jackets brushed clean, and that the garters that hold up their stockings aren't too flashy. Tell them to curtsy with their left legs and not to dare to touch a hair on the tail of my master's horse until they have kissed Petruchio's and Katherina's hands. Are they all ready?

Curtis   They are.

Grumio   Call them here.

Curtis   [*shouting to other servants*] Hey, do you hear me? You have to greet our master and face our mistress.

Grumio   Why, she has her own face.

Curtis   Who doesn't know that?

Grumio   Thou, it seems, that calls for company to
countenance her.

104 **Curtis**   I call them forth to credit her.

Enter four or five **Servingmen**.

Grumio   Why, she comes to borrow nothing of them.

Nathaniel   Welcome home, Grumio!

Phillip   How now, Grumio!

Joseph   What, Grumio!

Nicholas   Fellow Grumio!

110 **Nathaniel**   How now, old lad?

Grumio   Welcome, you; how now, you; what,
you; fellow, you—and thus much for greeting.
Now, my spruce companions, is all ready, and
all things neat?

Nathaniel   All things is ready. How near is our
116   master?

Grumio   E'en at hand, alighted by this; and therefore be Not—Cock's passion, silence! I hear my
master.

Enter **Petruchio** *and* **Kate**.

120 **Petruchio**   Where be these knaves? What, no man at door
To hold my stirrup, nor to take my horse?
Where is Nathaniel, Gregory, Philip?

All servants   Here, here, sir, here, sir.

Grumio   You don't, apparently, since you're calling for the servants to "face" her.

Curtis   I'm calling them here to give her credit [*that is, to honor her*].

Grumio   [*deliberately misunderstanding him*] Why, she doesn't need to borrow money from them.

[*Several servants enter.*]

Nathaniel   Welcome home, Grumio!

Philip   How's it going, Grumio?

Joseph   Hi, Grumio!

Nicholas   Grumio, my pal!

Grumio   [*greeting his fellow-servants one-by-one, shaking hands and slapping them on their backs*] Hello, you! . . . How are you? . . . Hi, there! . . . Hey, pal! . . . So much for greetings. Now, my fine friends, is everything ready and all straightened up?

Nathaniel   All things is ready. [**Nathaniel's** *ungrammatical speech reflects his lack of eduction.*] How soon will our master be here?

Grumio   He's almost here, probably getting off his horse right now, so don't—Oh, my God, be quiet! I hear him!

[**Petruchio** *and* **Katherina** *enter.*]

Petruchio   [*shouting*] Where are those rascals? What, no one is at the door to hold my stirrup or take my horse? Where is Nathaniel? Where is Gregory? Where is Philip?

All Servants   Here, sir! Here, sir!

Petruchio   Here, sir! here, sir! here, sir! here, sir!
125   You loggerheaded and unpolish'd grooms!
        What? no attendance? no regard? no duty?
        Where is the foolish knave I sent before?

Grumio   Here, sir, as foolish as I was before.

Petruchio   You peasant swain, you whoreson malt-horse
            drudge!
130   Did I not bid thee meet me in the park,
        And bring along these rascal knaves with thee?

Grumio   Nathaniel's coat, sir, was not fully made,
        And Gabr'el's pumps were all unpink'd i' th' heel;
134   There was no link to color Peter's hat,
        And Walter's dagger was not come from sheathing;
        There were none fine but Adam, Rafe, and Gregory;
        The rest were ragged, old, and beggarly,
        Yet, as they are, here are they come to meet you.

Petruchio   Go, rascals, go, and fetch my supper in.

Exeunt Servants.

[*Sings.*]

140   "Where is the life that late I led?
        Where are those?"—
        Sit down, Kate, and welcome. Soud, soud, soud, soud!

Enter **Servants** *with supper.*

        Why, when, I say? Nay, good sweet Kate, be merry.
        Off with my boots, you rogues! You villains, when?

[*Sings.*]

145   "It was the friar of orders grey,

Petruchio [*mockingly echoing them*] "Here, sir! Here, sir! Here, sir! Here, sir!" You block-headed, ill-mannered fools! What, is there no one to wait on us? To attend to us? To serve us? Where is the stupid scoundrel I sent on ahead?

Grumio Here I am, sir, just as stupid as I was before.

Petruchio You low-class peasant! You wretched, plodding bastard! Didn't I order you to meet me outside and bring these dim-witted scoundrels with you?

Grumio Sir, Nathaniel's coat wasn't finished and Gabriel's shoes needed the heels repaired, Peter's hat needed to be re-dyed and Walter's dagger was stuck in its sheath. None of them was ready except Adam, Ralph, and Gregory. The rest were ragged, worn out, and bedraggled. Yet here they are, in whatever condition, come to meet you.

Petruchio Go, you rascals, go and bring my supper in.

[*The servants hurry off to obey his orders.*]

[*singing loudly*] "Where is the life I used to lead?

Where are those—"

[*to* **Katherina**] Sit down, Kate, and make yourself at home.

[*shouting and pounding on the table with his fist*] Food! Food! Food! Food!

[**Servants** *come running in with supper.*]

[*to* **Servants**] Why, what took you so long?

[*to* **Katherina**] Now, dear sweet Kate, be happy—

[*to* **Servants**] Pull off my boots, you rogues! You scoundrels, hurry!

[*singing again*] "It was a priest in robes of gray

179

As he forth walked on his way"—
Out, you rogue, you pluck my foot awry.
Take that, and mend the plucking [off] the other.

[*Strikes him.*]

Be merry, Kate. Some water here; what ho!

Enter one with water.

Where's my spaniel Troilus? Sirrah, get you hence,
151   And bid my cousin Ferdinand come hither;
One, Kate, that you must kiss, and be acquainted with.
Where are my slippers? Shall I have some water?
Come, Kate, and wash, and welcome heartily.
155   You whoreson villain, will you let it fall?

[*Strikes him.*]

Katherina   Patience, I pray you, 'twas a fault unwilling.

Petruchio   A whoreson, beetle-headed, flap-ear'd knave!
Come, Kate, sit down, I know you have a stomach.
Will you give thanks, sweet Kate, or else shall I?
What's this? Mutton?

1st Servingman   Ay.

Petruchio   Who brought it?

160 **Peter**   I.

And as he walked along his way — "

[to a **Servant**] Stop, you fool! You're twisting my foot. Take that, and do better with pulling off the next one! [**Petruchio** hits him.]

[to **Katherina**] Cheer up, Kate. [She stands off to the side, looking exhausted and miserable.]

[to a **Servant**] Bring some water here, I say! Hey! Where is my spaniel Troilus? Go, boy, and tell my cousin Ferdinand to come here.

[to **Katherina**] Kate, you will want to give him a friendly kiss in greeting and get to know him better. [No explanation is given, but **Petruchio's** cousin never appears nor is he mentioned again in the play.]

[shouting impatiently to **Servants**] Where are my slippers? Where is the water?

[A **Servant** enters with water for washing.]

[to **Katherina**] Come, Kate, wash up. You are warmly welcomed.

[to **Servant**] You villainous bastard! You spilled it! [**Petruchio** hits him.]

Katherina   Please, don't be angry! He didn't do it on purpose.

Petruchio   He's a block-headed, jug-eared bastard! Come sit down, Kate. I know you must be hungry. Will you ask the blessing, sweet Kate, or shall I?

[As she prepares to do so, he shouts at the **Servants**.] What is this? Mutton?

First Servant   [quavering in fear] Y-yes.

Petruchio   Who brought it?

Peter   [also fearfully] I d-did.   181

Petruchio   'Tis burnt, and so is all the meat.
What dogs are these? Where is the rascal cook?
How durst you, villains, bring it from the dresser
And serve it thus to me that love it not?
165   There, take it to you, trenchers, cups, and all.

[*He throws down the table and meat and all, and beats them.*]

You heedless joltheads and unmanner'd slaves!
What, do you grumble? I'll be with you straight.

[*Exeunt Servants.*]

Katherina   I pray you, husband, be not so disquiet.
The meat was well, if you were so contented.

Petruchio   I tell thee, Kate, 'twas burnt and dried away,
171   And I expressly am forbid to touch it;
For it engenders choler, planteth anger,
And better 'twere that both of us did fast,
Since of ourselves, ourselves are choleric,
175   Than feed it with such overroasted flesh.
Be patient, to-morrow't shall be mended,
And for this night we'll fast for company.
Come, I will bring thee to thy bridal chamber.

Exeunt.

Enter **Servants** *severally.*

Nathaniel   Peter, didst ever see the like?

180   **Peter**   He kills her in her own humor.

Enter **Curtis**, *a servant.*

Grumio   Where is he?

182

Petruchio   It's burnt! And so is all the meat! You low-down dogs! Where is that no-good cook? How dare you, you villains, bring it from the sideboard and serve it like this to me? There! Take it away, plates and cups and everything!

[*He throws the food, dishes, and utensils all over the room.*]

You careless blockheads and uncouth slaves! What, do you dare to grumble? I'll deal with you in a minute.

[*The* **Servants** *leave.*]

Katherina   [*distraught to see the food spoiled*] Please, husband, don't be so angry! The meat was fine, if you would be willing to be satisfied with it.

Petruchio   I tell you, Kate, it was burnt and dried out. I'm not allowed to eat burnt meat because it causes irritability and anger. It would be better that neither of us eat tonight, since we're naturally inclined to be hot-tempered, than feed our bad tempers with over-cooked meat. Be patient. It will be better tomorrow, and for tonight, we will fast together. Come, I will take you to the bridal chamber. [*At one time, people believed that a person's mood and health were controlled by the four bodily fluids, known as "humors": black bile, yellow bile, blood, and phlegm. An excess of yellow bile (choler) was thought to cause anger.*]

[**Petruchio** *and* **Katherina** *leave, as she looks back longingly. The* **Servants** *re-enter from various doorways.*]

Nathaniel   Peter, did you ever see anything like it?

Peter   He's giving her a taste of her own medicine.

[**Curtis** *re-enters.*]

Grumio   [*whispering to others*] Where is he?

Curtis In her chamber, making a sermon of continency
    to her,
And rails, and swears, and rates, that she, poor soul,
185 Knows not which way to stand, to look, to speak,
And sits as one new risen from a dream.
Away, away, for he is coming hither.

                                   [*Exeunt.*]

Enter **Petruchio**.

Petruchio Thus have I politicly begun my reign,
And 'tis my hope to end successfully.
190 My falcon now is sharp and passing empty,
And till she stoop, she must not be full-gorg'd,
For then she never looks upon her lure.
Another way I have to man my haggard,
To make her come, and know her keeper's call,
195 That is, to watch her, as we watch these kites
That bate and beat and will not be obedient.
She eat no meat to-day, nor none shall eat;
Last night she slept not, nor to-night she shall not;
As with the meat, some undeserved fault
200 I'll find about the making of the bed,
And here I'll fling the pillow, there the bolster,
This way the coverlet, another way the sheets.
Ay, and amid this hurly I intend
That all is done in reverend care of her,
205 And in conclusion, she shall watch all night,
And if she chance to nod I'll rail and brawl,
And with the clamor keep her still awake.
This is a way to kill a wife with kindness,
And thus I'll curb her mad and headstrong humor.
210 He that knows better how to tame a shrew,
Now let him speak; 'tis charity to shew.

                                   Exit.

Curtis   In her bedroom, preaching to her about self-control.
He's yelling and swearing and scolding, and she, poor
thing, doesn't know how she should stand, or look at him,
or speak to him, so she just sits like someone who has just
woken up from a dream.

[*Hearing approaching footsteps, he shoos his fellow servants away.*] Go! Go! He's coming!

[*The* **Servants** *scurry away as* **Petruchio** *re-enters.*]

Petruchio   [*rubbing his hands together in satisfaction*] And
so I have cleverly begun my dominance, and I hope to end
it successfully. My falcon [*that is,* **Katherina**] is now famished and unfed, and until she is willing to obey orders, she
must not be allowed to satisfy her hunger or she will not be
controllable. Another way I intend to tame my hawk, to
make her come to me and obey my commands, is to keep
an eye on her as trainers do with birds that won't follow
orders, making sure that she eats nothing today, nor shall
anyone else eat. Also, last night she didn't get any sleep,
nor shall she tonight. As with the food, I'll find some supposed problem with the bed. I'll fling the pillow here, and
the bolster there, the quilt this way and the sheets another.
Yes, and I will claim that all this uproar is done out of my
tender care for her, with the result that she will stay awake
all night. And if she happens to nod off, I'll shout and carry
on, keeping her awake with the noise. This is how I'll kill my
wife with kindness, and so I will restrain her wild and headstrong nature. If anyone knows a better way to tame a
shrew, let him speak up out of kindness to his fellow man.

[**Petruchio** *leaves.*]

Scene 2

Enter **Tranio** [*as Lucentio*] *and* **Hortensio** [*as Litio*].

Tranio   Is't possible, friend Litio, that Mistress Bianca
Doth fancy any other but Lucentio?
I tell you, sir, she bears me fair in hand.

Hortensio   Sir, to satisfy you in what I have said,
5   Stand by and mark the manner of his teaching.

[*They stand aside.*]

Enter **Bianca** [*and* **Lucentio** *as Cambio*].

Lucentio   Now, mistress, profit you in what you read?

Bianca   What, master, read you? First resolve me that.

Lucentio   I read that I profess, the Art to Love.

Bianca   And may you prove, sir, master of your art!

10 **Lucentio**   While you, sweet dear, prove mistress of my heart!

[*They retire.*]

Hortensio   Quick proceeders, marry! Now tell me, I pray,
You that durst swear that your mistress Bianca
Lov'd [none] in the world so well as Lucentio.

Tranio   O despiteful love, unconstant womankind!
15   I tell thee, Litio, this is wonderful.

Scene 2

In front of **Baptista's** *house.*

[**Tranio,** *disguised as* **Lucentio**, *and* **Hortensio,** *as* **Licio,** *enter.*]

Tranio   Is it possible, my friend Licio, that Bianca could prefer anyone else to me? I assure you, sir, that she appears to favor me.

Hortensio   Sir, to prove to you what I've said, stand over here and watch the way he acts when he is teaching her.

[**Tranio** *and* **Hortensio** *hide themselves.*]

Lucentio   [*disguised as* **Cambio**] Now, miss, are you benefiting from your reading?

Bianca   [*flirtatiously*] What do you read, professor? Tell me that first.

Lucentio   I read what I also teach: *The Art of Love.* [*Ovid's* The Art of Love *was a how-to manual on seduction.*]

Bianca   I hope you will turn out to be an expert in your subject, sir!

Lucentio   And you, sweetheart, are the queen of my heart.

Hortensio   [*whispering bitterly to* **Tranio**] They're certainly making quick progress! Now, tell me, do you still swear that Bianca loves no one else in the world so well as Lucentio?

Tranio   [*feigning indignation*] Oh, cruel lover! Faithless womanhood! I'm telling you, Licio, this is unbelievable!

Hortensio   Mistake no more, I am not Litio,
Nor a musician, as I seem to be,
But one that scorn to live in this disguise
For such a one as leaves a gentleman,
20 And makes a god of such a cullion.
Know, sir, that I am call'd Hortensio.

Tranio   Signior Hortensio, I have often heard
Of your entire affection to Bianca,
And since mine eyes are witness of her lightness,
25 I will with you, if you be so contented,
Forswear Bianca and her love for ever.

Hortensio   See how they kiss and court! Signior Lucentio,
Here is my hand, and here I firmly vow
Never to woo her more, but do forswear her
30 As one unworthy all the former favors
That I have fondly flatter'd [her] withal.

Tranio   And here I take the like unfeigned oath,
Never to marry with her though she would entreat.
Fie on her, see how beastly she doth court him!

35 **Hortensio**   Would all the world but he had quite forsworn!
For me, that I may surely keep mine oath,
I will be married to a wealthy widow,
Ere three days pass, which hath as long lov'd me
As I have lov'd this proud disdainful haggard.
40 And so farewell, Signior Lucentio.
Kindness in women, not their beauteous looks,
Shall win my love, and so I take my leave,
In resolution as I swore before.

[*Exit.*]

Hortensio   I won't deceive you any longer. I am not Licio, nor am I a musician, as I appear to be. I refuse to wear this disguise any longer for someone who would reject a gentleman and worship such a low-class scoundrel. [*He pulls off his false beard, throwing it to the ground in disgust.*] My name, sir, is Hortensio.

Tranio   Signior Hortensio, I have often heard of your deep love for Bianca. Now that I've seen with my own eyes just how fickle she is, I will, if you don't mind, join you in renouncing Bianca and her love forever.

Hortensio   Look at how they kiss and cuddle! Signior Lucentio, let's shake hands on this unwavering promise: I now swear to you that I will not court her anymore. I completely reject her as someone undeserving of all the gifts I have foolishly given her to win her love.

Tranio   And I swear never to marry her, not even if she should beg me. Curses upon her! Look how disgustingly she snuggles with him!

Hortensio   I wish that the whole world except for him had given up on her! As for me, to make sure that I keep my vow, before three days have passed I will be married to a wealthy widow who has loved me as long as I have loved this proud, stuck-up woman! And so goodbye, Signior Lucentio. Good treatment from a woman and not good looks will win my love. And so I will leave you, determined to do as I have vowed. [*By saying that he wishes that the whole world had given up on* **Bianca**, **Hortensio** *means that he hopes she will end up an old maid, in that he doesn't believe she will marry a penniless tutor such as* **Cambio** *appears to be.*]

[**Hortensio** *leaves in a huff.*]

Tranio   Mistress Bianca, bless you with such grace
45   As 'longeth to a lover's blessed case!
Nay, I have ta'en you napping, gentle love,
And have forsworn you with Hortensio.

Bianca   Tranio, you jest, but have you both forsworn me?

Tranio   Mistress, we have.

Lucentio   Then we are rid of Litio.

50   **Tranio**   I' faith, he'll have a lusty widow now,
That shall be woo'd and wedded in a day.

Bianca   God give him joy!

Tranio   Ay, and he'll tame her.

Bianca   He says so, Tranio?

Tranio   Faith, he is gone unto the taming-school.

55   **Bianca**   The taming-school! what, is there such a place?

Tranio   Ay, mistress, and Petruchio is the master,
That teacheth tricks eleven and twenty long,
To tame a shrew and charm her chattering tongue.

Enter **Biondello**.

Biondello   O master, master, I have watch'd so long
60   That I am dog-weary, but at last I spied
An ancient angel coming down the hill,
Will serve the turn.

Tranio   What is he, Biondello?

Tranio   [*revealing his presence to* **Lucentio** *and* **Bianca**,
and speaking as himself] My lady Bianca, may you be
blessed with all the good fortune of a successful lover! No,
I've caught you napping, dear love, and have renounced
you, as has Hortensio.

Bianca   [*clapping her hands in delight*] Tranio, you're
kidding! Have you both really renounced me? [*She includes
the false "***Lucentio***" as a lover whom she is happy to be
rid of.*]

Tranio   [*sweeping her a formal bow*] Mistress, we have.

Lucentio   Then we're rid of "Licio."

Tranio   In fact, he's going after a lusty widow now. He plans
to woo and wed her in one day.

Bianca   [*giggling*] May God give him happiness!

Tranio   Yes, and he's going to "tame" her.

Bianca   [*skeptically*] Or so he says, Tranio.

Tranio   Yes, he's gone to the taming school.

Bianca   The "taming school"? Is there such a place?

Tranio   Yes, my lady, and Petruchio is the teacher. He
teaches every trick in the book to tame a shrew and silence
her ranting tongue.

[**Biondello** *enters.*]

Biondello   Master! Master! I've been watching so long that
I'm dog-tired, but I finally saw a good old fellow coming
down the hill who will suit our needs.

Tranio   Who is he, Biondello?

Biondello   Master, a mercantant, or a pedant,
I know not what, but formal in apparel,
65   In gait and countenance surely like a father.

Lucentio   And what of him, Tranio?

Tranio   If he be credulous, and trust my tale,
I'll make him glad to seem Vincentio,
And give assurance to Baptista Minola,
70   As if he were the right Vincentio.
Take [in] your love, and then let me alone.

[Exeunt Lucentio and Bianca.]

Enter a **Pedant**.

Pedant   God save you, sir!

Tranio   And you, sir! you are welcome.
Travel you far on, or are you at the farthest?

Pedant   Sir, at the farthest for a week or two,
75   But then up farther, and as far as Rome,
And so to Tripoli, if God lend me life.

Tranio   What countryman, I pray?

Pedant   Of Mantua.

Tranio   Of Mantua, sir? marry, God forbid!
And come to Padua, careless of your life?

Pedant   My life, sir! How, I pray? for that goes hard.

81   **Tranio**   'Tis death for any one in Mantua
To come to Padua. Know you not the cause?
Your ships are stay'd at Venice, and the Duke,
For private quarrel 'twixt your Duke and him,
85   Hath publish'd and proclaim'd it openly.
'Tis marvel, but that you are but newly come,
You might have heard it else proclaim'd about.

Biondello   A merchant or a teacher, master. I don't know. But he is decently dressed, and he looks and acts like just a father.

Lucentio   And what about him, Tranio?

Tranio   If he is easily tricked and believes my story, I'll make him happy to pretend to be Vincentio. Take your sweetheart inside and leave me alone here.

[**Lucentio** and **Bianca** leave. The **Pedant** enters.]

Pedant   [bowing to **Tranio**, disguised as **Lucentio**] Good day to you, sir.

Tranio   [bowing] And to you, sir! You are welcome here. Are you traveling farther, or have you reached your destination?

Pedant   This is as far as I go for a week or two, sir. But then I will move on, eventually going to Rome and, from there, to Tripoli, God willing.

Tranio   Where are you from, sir?

Pedant   Mantua.

Tranio   [pretending to be horrified] Mantua, sir? Good God, no! And you have come to Padua, disregarding the danger to your life that doing so puts you in?

Pedant   [shocked and concerned] My life, sir! What can you mean? That's a shocking thing to say.

Tranio   [looking around and lowering his voice as if afraid of being overheard] Anyone from Mantua who comes to Padua is risking his life. Don't you know the reason? Because of a personal quarrel between your duke and him, the duke of Padua has issued public orders that all ships from Mantua are to be detained at Venice. I'm amazed that you haven't heard, but since you have only just arrived I suppose that you haven't heard the public proclamations yet.

Pedant Alas, sir, it is worse for me than so,
For I have bills for money by exchange
90   From Florence, and must here deliver them.

Tranio Well, sir, to do you courtesy,
This will I do, and this I will advise you.
First, tell me, have you ever been at Pisa?

Pedant Ay, sir, in Pisa have I often been,
95   Pisa renowned for grave citizens.

Tranio Among them know you one Vincentio?

Pedant I know him not, but I have heard of him;
A merchant of incomparable wealth.

Tranio He is my father, sir, and sooth to say,
100   In count'nance somewhat doth resemble you.

Biondello [*Aside.*] As much as an apple doth an
oyster, and all one.

Tranio To save your life in this extremity,
This favor will I do you for his sake;
105   And think it not the worst of all your fortunes
That you are like to Sir Vincentio.
His name and credit shall you undertake,
And in my house you shall be friendly lodg'd.
Look that you take upon you as you should;
110   You understand me, sir? So shall you stay
Till you have done your business in the city.
If this be court'sy, sir, accept of it.

Pedant O sir, I do, and will repute you ever
The patron of my life and liberty.

194

Pedant   Oh, my! Sir, it's even worse for me than you think. I have promissory notes from Florence and I must deliver them here.

Tranio   [*shaking his head as if worried, but then pretending to be struck by inspiration*] Well, sir, to do you a favor, this is what I will do and what I advise you to do. But first tell me if you have ever been to Pisa.

Pedant   Yes, sir, I've often been to Pisa which is famous for its influential citizens.

Tranio   Do you know Vincentio?

Pedant   No, I don't know him, but I've heard of him. He's a fabulously wealthy businessman.

Tranio   He is my father, sir, and to tell you the truth, you do resemble him somewhat.

Biondello   [*under his breath*] As much as an apple resembles an oyster, but so what?

Tranio   To save your life in this dire situation, I'll do you this favor for his sake—and don't think that it's bad luck that you look like Signior Vincentio. You shall assume his name and reputation, and I will gladly allow you to live in my house. Just act as you should under the circumstances. Do you understand me, sir? [*The* **Pedant** *nods vehemently.*] In this way, you may stay in the city until you have completed your business. Please allow me to do this kindness for you, sir.

Pedant   [*vigorously shaking* **Tranio's** *hand*] Oh, sir, I will! And I will forever consider you to be the protector of my life and freedom.

Tranio   Then go with me to make the matter good.

116   This by the way I let you understand:
My father is here look'd for every day,
To pass assurance of a dow'r in marriage
'Twixt me and one Baptista's daughter here.

120   In all these circumstances I'll instruct you;
Go with me to clothe you as becomes you.

Exeunt.

Scene 3

Enter **Katherina** *and* **Grumio**.

Grumio   No, no, forsooth I dare not for my life.

Katherina   The more my wrong, the more his spite appears.
What, did he marry me to famish me?
Beggars that come unto my father's door

5   Upon entreaty have a present alms,
If not, elsewhere they meet with charity;
But I, who never knew how to entreat,
Nor never needed that I should entreat,
Am starv'd for meat, giddy for lack of sleep,

10   With oaths kept waking, and with brawling fed;
And that which spites me more than all these wants,
He does it under name of perfect love;
As who should say, if I should sleep or eat,
'Twere deadly sickness, or else present death.

15   I prithee go, and get me some repast;
I care not what, so it be wholesome food.

Tranio   Then come with me to put the plan in action. By the way, I must tell you that my father is expected to arrive any day to give guarantees of a marriage dowry between me and one of Baptista's daughters. I'll tell you all about it. Come with me so that we can dress you in the way you should look as Vincentio.

[*They leave.*]

Scene 3

A room in **Petruchio's** *house.*

[**Katherina** *and* **Grumio** *enter, arguing.*]

Grumio   No, no, I tell you! He would kill me!

Katherina   The more I endure, the more spiteful he becomes! Did he marry me just to starve me? When beggars come to my father's door, they are immediately given charity. And if they don't get it there, they can get it elsewhere. Yet I, who have never even known how to beg much less had to do so, am starved for food, dizzy from lack of sleep, kept awake by his cursing, and fed nothing but his arguing. And what makes it even worse, he claims he does it all out of love! He says that if I were to sleep or eat, it would cause me to become deathly ill or even die. I beg of you, go and get me something to eat! I don't care what it is as long as it's nutritious.

Grumio   What say you to a neat's foot?

Katherina   'Tis passing good, I prithee let me have it.

Grumio   I fear it is too choleric a meat.
20   How say you to a fat tripe finely broil'd?

Katherina   I like it well, good Grumio, fetch it me.

Grumio   I cannot tell, I fear 'tis choleric.
What say you to a piece of beef and mustard?

Katherina   A dish that I do love to feed upon.

25 **Grumio**   Ay, but the mustard is too hot a little.

Katherina   Why then the beef, and let the mustard rest.

Grumio   Nay then I will not, you shall have the mustard,
Or else you get no beef of Grumio.

Katherina   Then both or one, or any thing thou wilt.

30 **Grumio**   Why then the mustard without the beef.

Katherina   Go get thee gone, thou false deluding slave,

Beats him.

That feed'st me with the very name of meat.
Sorrow on thee and all the pack of you
That triumph thus upon my misery!
35   Go get thee gone, I say.

Enter **Petruchio** *and* **Hortensio** *with meat.*

Petruchio   How fares my Kate? What, sweeting, all amort?

Grumio   Would you like a cooked ox foot?

Katherina   That would be fine. Please, let me have it.

Grumio   [*shaking his head doubtfully*] I'm afraid that's too likely to increase your choler [*that is, the yellow bile which was believed to cause a hot temper*]. What would you say to a big piece of ox stomach, nicely broiled?

Katherina   I would love it. Dear Grumio, please get it for me.

Grumio   [*shaking his head again*] I don't know. I'm afraid that it would make your hot temper worse. What would you say to a piece of beef with mustard?

Katherina   [*eagerly*] It's something I love to eat.

Grumio   Yes, but the mustard would be too hot [*and thus would increase her "choler"*].

Katherina   Then just bring the beef and leave the mustard off.

Grumio   No, I won't do it. You must have the mustard or else you will get no beef from me.

Katherina   [*in exasperation*] Then bring both or either one, or anything you want.

Grumio   Why, then, I'll bring the mustard without the beef.

Katherina   [*realizing that he has no intention of complying with her requests*] Go! Get out of here, you lying, deceiving scoundrel! [*She beats him.*] You feed me with nothing but the word "meat." Shame on you and all the rest of you who gloat over my misery! Go on! Get out of here, I tell you!

[**Petruchio** *and* **Hortensio** *enter, bringing meat.*]

Petruchio   How are you, my Kate? What, sweetie, are you feeling down?

Hortensio   Mistress, what cheer?

Katherina   Faith, as cold as can be.

Petruchio   Pluck up thy spirits, look cheerfully upon me.
Here, love, thou seest how diligent I am
40   To dress thy meat myself, and bring it thee.
I am sure, sweet Kate, this kindness merits thanks.
What, not a word? Nay then, thou lov'st it not;
And all my pains is sorted to no proof.
Here, take away this dish.

Katherina   I pray you let it stand.

Petruchio   The poorest service is repaid with thanks,
46   And so shall mine before you touch the meat.

Katherina   I thank you, sir.

Hortensio   Signior Petruchio, fie, you are to blame.
Come, Mistress Kate, I'll bear you company.

Petruchio   [*Aside.*] Eat it up all, Hortensio, if thou
50   lovest me.—
Much good do it unto thy gentle heart!
Kate, eat apace. And now, my honey love,
Will we return unto thy father's house,
And revel it as bravely as the best,
55   With silken coats and caps, and golden rings,
With ruffs and cuffs, and fardingales and things,
With scarfs and fans, and double change of brav'ry,
With amber bracelets, beads, and all this knav'ry.
What, hast thou din'd? The tailor stays thy leisure,
60   To deck thy body with his ruffling treasure.

Enter **Tailor**.

Hortensio   [*bowing to* **Katherina**] How are you, madam?

Katherina   Actually, I'm as cold as can be [*as opposed to being hot-tempered or choleric*].

Petruchio   Cheer up. Smile at me. [*He lifts her drooping chin with one hand, but she pulls away.*] Look, darling, I have actually prepared your meat myself and brought it to you. I'm sure, sweet Kate, that this kindness deserves thanks. [*She is too angry to reply, so he continues.*] What, not a word? No, then I guess you don't want it, and all my effort is for nothing.

[*to* **Servant**] Here, take way this dish.

Katherina   I beg you, let it stay.

Petruchio   The most insignificant favor is repaid with thanks, and my favor to you shall receive thanks before you touch the meat.

Katherina   [*whispering*] Thank you, sir.

Hortensio   For shame, Signior Petruchio! You are at fault. Come, my lady Katherina, I'll join you while you eat.

Petruchio   [*whispering to* **Hortensio**] If you are my friend, Hortensio, you'll eat it all up.

[*to* **Katherina**] May it do your gentle heart good, Kate. Eat quickly, my sweet love, for we will now return to your father's house and celebrate as splendidly as the best of them, wearing silk coats and hats and golden rings, frills and fancy cuffs, and even lavish underwear and everything. We'll have sashes and fans and two changes of clothes, amber bracelets, beads, and all kinds of finery. What, are you finished eating? The tailor [*that is, dressmaker*] awaits you in order to dress your body with his be-ruffled splendor.

[The **Tailor** *enters*.]

Come, tailor, let us see these ornaments;
Lay forth the gown.

Enter **Haberdasher.**

What news with you, sir?

Haberdasher   Here is the cap your worship did bespeak.

Petruchio   Why, this was moulded on a porringer—
65   A velvet dish. Fie, fie, 'tis lewd and filthy.
Why, 'tis a cockle or a walnut-shell,
A knack, a toy, a trick, a baby's cap.
Away with it! come, let me have a bigger.

Katherina   I'll have no bigger, this doth fit the time,
70   And gentlewomen wear such caps as these.

Petruchio   When you are gentle, you shall have one too,
And not till then.

Hortensio   [*Aside.*] That will not be in haste.

Katherina   Why, sir, I trust I may have leave to speak,
And speak I will. I am no child, no babe;
75   Your betters have endur'd me say my mind,
And if you cannot, best you stop your ears.
My tongue will tell the anger of my heart,
Or else my heart concealing it will break,
And rather than it shall, I will be free,
80   Even to the uttermost, as I please, in words.

Petruchio   Why, thou say'st true; it is [a] paltry cap,
A custard-coffin, a bauble, a silken pie.
I love thee well, in that thou lik'st it not.

Come, Tailor, let's see the finery. Show us the gown.

[The **Haberdasher** *enters.*]

[*to* **Haberdasher**] What's new, sir?

Haberdasher   Here is the hat you ordered, your honor.

Petruchio   [*in disgust*] Why, this was patterned on a baby's bowl; it's a velvet "dish." Shame on you! It's vulgar and disgraceful! Why, it's nothing but the shell of an oyster or a walnut. It's junk, rubbish, a joke, a baby's bonnet! Take it away! Come, I want a bigger one.

Katherina   [*indignantly, trying unsuccessfully to snatch the hat out of* **Petruchio's** *hand*] I don't want a bigger one! This is in fashion, and gentlewomen wear hats like these.

Petruchio   When you are gentle, you shall have one, too, and not until then.

Hortensio   [*to himself*] That won't be any time soon.

Katherina   [*still more indignantly*] Why, sir, I suppose that I have your permission to speak, and speak I will! I'm not a child or a baby. Better people than you have had to hear me say what's on my mind, and if you can't stand it, you may plug your ears. I'll tell you just how angry I am, or else my heart will burst from trying to hold it in. And rather than have that happen, I will say everything I want to say, however I want to say it.

Petruchio   [*amiably, as if agreeing with* **Katherina**.] Why, you are correct; it is a pitiful excuse for a hat, a mere tart crust, a trifle, a pie made out of silk. I love you for disliking it.

203

Katherina   Love me, or love me not, I like the cap,
85   And it I will have, or I will have none.

[*Exit Haberdasher.*]

Petruchio   Thy gown? why, ay. Come, tailor, let us see't.
O mercy, God, what masquing stuff is here?
What's this? a sleeve? 'tis like [a] demi-cannon.
What, up and down carv'd like an apple-tart?
90   Here's snip and nip and cut and slish and slash,
Like to a censer in a barber's shop.
Why, what a' devil's name, tailor, call'st thou this?

Hortensio   [*Aside.*] I see she's like to have neither cap
nor gown.

Tailor   You bid me make it orderly and well,
95   According to the fashion and the time.

Petruchio   Marry, and did; but if you be rememb'red,
I did not bid you mar it to the time.
Go hop me over every kennel home,
For you shall hop without my custom, sir.
100   I'll none of it; hence, make your best of it.

Katherina   I never saw a better fashion'd gown,
More quaint, more pleasing, nor more commendable.
Belike you mean to make a puppet of me.

Petruchio   Why, true, he means to make a puppet of thee.

Tailor   She says your worship means to make
106   a puppet of her.

Katherina   [*angrily*] Whether or not you love me, I like the hat, and I will have it or I won't have any!

[*Shaking his head in confusion, the* **Haberdasher** *leaves, taking the hat with him.*]

Petruchio   [*pretending that* **Katherina** *has asked to see her dress*] Your dress? Why, yes!

Come along, Tailor, let's see it. [*When* **Petruchio** *sees the gown, his expression changes to one of disgust.*] God have mercy! What kind of costume is this? What's this? A sleeve? It looks like a cannon. What's this up and down part, carved up like an apple tart? Here's a snip and a nip, a cut and a slit and a slash, like a perfume censer in a barber shop. What in the devil's name, Tailor, do you call this?

Hortensio   [*to himself*] I see that she isn't likely to get either the hat or the dress.

Tailor   [*stammering in confusion and dismay*] Y-you told me to make it properly and well, in keeping with the current style.

Petruchio   Indeed I did, but if you recall I didn't tell you to make a mockery of the style. Go on, hop over every gutter on your way home, for you shall hop along without my business, sir. I won't have it. Go! Do what you want with it.

Katherina   [*protesting angrily*] I never saw a better-designed dress, or one more beautiful, more pleasing, or more attractive. I suppose you intend to make me into a dress-up doll.

Petruchio   [*as if agreeing with* **Katherina**] Why, that's true. He intends to make you look like a dress-up doll.

Tailor   [*timidly, attempting to correct* **Petruchio's** *apparent misunderstanding*] She is saying that you, your worship, intend to make a dress-up doll out of her.

Petruchio   O monstrous arrogance! Thou liest, thou
  thread, thou thimble,
 Thou yard, three-quarters, half-yard, quarter, nail!
 Thou flea, thou nit, thou winter-cricket thou!
 Brav'd in mine own house with a skein of thread?
111 Away, thou rag, thou quantity, thou remnant,
 Or I shall so bemete thee with thy yard
 As thou shalt think on prating whilst thou liv'st!
 I tell thee, I, that thou hast marr'd her gown.

Tailor   Your worship is deceiv'd, the gown is made
116 Just as my master had direction.
 Grumio gave order how it should be done.

Grumio   I gave him no order, I gave him the stuff.

Tailor   But how did you desire it should be made?

120 **Grumio**   Marry, sir, with needle and thread.

Tailor   But did you not request to have it cut?

Grumio   Thou hast fac'd many things.

123 **Tailor**   I have.

Grumio   Face not me; thou hast brav'd many men,
brave not me; I will neither be fac'd nor brav'd. I
say unto thee, I bid thy master cut out the gown,
but I did not bid him cut it to pieces: *Ergo*, thou
liest.

Tailor   Why, here is the note of the fashion to
130 testify.

Petruchio   Read it.

Petruchio   [*roaring*] Oh, the unbelievable arrogance! You're lying, you piece of thread, you thimble, you yard, three-quarters, half-yard, quarter, you little snippet of fabric! You flea, you egg of a louse, you winter cricket, you! Defied in my own house by a spool of thread? Leave, you rag, you fragment, you remnant, or I will "measure" you with your own yardstick so that you will remember it for the rest of your life! I tell you, you have destroyed her gown.

Tailor   Your worship is mistaken. The gown is made just as my master was instructed. Grumio ordered how it should look.

Grumio   I didn't give him orders. I gave him the fabric.

Tailor   But how did you want it to be made?

Grumio   [*deliberately misunderstanding him*] Why, sir, with needle and thread.

Tailor   But didn't you ask to have it cut out?

Grumio   You have faced many things.

Tailor   [*He assumes that **Grumio** means that he has applied a fancy edging to many garments.*] I have.

Grumio   [**Grumio** *switches to the other definition of "faced," meaning to "confront."*] You won't face me! You may have clothed many men, but you won't defy me. [*He's punning on the two meanings for "to brave": to clothe and to defy.*] I won't be confronted or defied. I tell you that I instructed your master to cut out the dress, but I didn't tell him to cut it to pieces, so you lie!

Tailor   Why, here is the written order for the gown. [*He takes out a piece of paper.*]

Petruchio   Read it.

Grumio   The note lies in 's throat if he say I said so.

Tailor   [*Reads.*] "*Inprimis*, a loose-bodied gown"—

Grumio   Master, if ever I said loose-bodied gown,
sew me in the skirts of it, and beat me to death with
137   a bottom of brown thread. I said a gown.

Petruchio   Proceed.

Tailor   [*Reads.*] "With a small compass'd cape"—

140 **Grumio**   I confess the cape.

Tailor   [*Reads.*] "With a trunk sleeve"—

Grumio   I confess two sleeves.

Tailor   [*Reads.*] "The sleeves curiously cut."—

144 **Petruchio**   Ay, there's the villainy.

Grumio   Error i' th' bill, sir, error i' th' bill! I commanded the sleeves should be cut out, and sew'd up
again, and that I'll prove upon thee, though thy little
finger be arm'd in a thimble.

Tailor   This is true that I say; an I had thee in
150   place where, thou shouldst know it.

Grumio   I am for thee straight. Take thou the bill,
give me thy mete-yard, and spare not me.

Hortensio   God-a-mercy, Grumio, then he shall have
154   no odds.

Grumio   The note lies through its teeth if it says I said so.

Tailor   [*reading from paper*] "First, a loose-bodied gown—"

Grumio   Master, if I ever said "loose-bodied gown," you may sew me into its skirts and beat me to death with a reel of brown thread. I said "a gown."

Petruchio   [*to* **Tailor**] Continue.

Tailor   [*continues reading*] "With a small, flared cape—"

Grumio   I admit to the cape.

Tailor   [*continues reading*] "With a full sleeve—"

Grumio   I admit two sleeves.

Tailor   [*continues reading*] "The sleeves ornately cut—"

Petruchio   Ah, that's where the problem is.

Grumio   Error in the bill, sir! Error in the bill! I ordered that the sleeves be cut out and sewed up again, and I'll fight you to prove it, even if your little finger is armed with your thimble! [*He raises his fists in classic boxing stance, while the* **Tailor**, *alarmed, steps back a pace.*]

Tailor   [*haughtily, as if unwilling to behave in so undignified a way*] What I've said is true, and if I had you in the right place, you would know it.

Grumio   [*dancing in place, as boxers do*] I'll fight you right now! You use a real weapon, I'll use your yard-stick, and don't hold back in the fight.

Hortensio   [*laughing at* **Grumio's** *pugnacity*] Merciful God, Grumio! He won't stand a chance!

Petruchio   Well, sir, in brief, the gown is not for me.

Grumio   You are i' th' right, sir, 'tis for my mistress.

Petruchio   Go, take it up unto thy master's use.

Grumio   Villain, not for thy life! Take up my mistress'
gown for thy master's use!

160 **Petruchio**   Why, sir, what's your conceit in that?

Grumio   O, sir, the conceit is deeper than you think for:
Take up my mistress' gown to his master's use!
O fie, fie, fie!

Petruchio   [*Aside.*] Hortensio, say thou wilt see the
tailor paid.—
165 Go take it hence, be gone, and say no more.

Hortensio   Tailor, I'll pay thee for thy gown to-morrow,
Take no unkindness of his hasty words.
Away, I say, commend me to thy master.

Exit Tailor.

Petruchio   Well, sir, to be brief, the gown is not for me.

Grumio   [*taking* **Petruchio** *literally*] You're right, sir; it's for my mistress.

Petruchio   Go, take it back for your master to use.

Grumio   [*to* **Tailor**] Villain, not on your life! You can't let your master lift up my mistress' gown! [**Grumio** *implies that the* **Tailor's** *master and* **Katherina** *would be sexually involved.*]

Petruchio   What is your conception, sir, of the problem?

Grumio   Oh, sir, the conception is much worse than you think if he is fooling around under my mistress' gown! Oh, shame, shame, shame!

Petruchio   [*softly*] Hortensio, tell the tailor that you will see that he is paid.

[*to* **Tailor**] Take it away! Go on! And don't say another word!

Hortensio   [*quietly so that only the* **Tailor** *can hear*] Tailor, I'll pay you for the gown tomorrow. Don't be offended by his harsh words. [*with impatience and more loudly so that all can hear*] Go, I tell you! [*quietly again*] Greet your master for me.

[*The* **Tailor** *leaves, shaking his head in confusion.*]

211

Petruchio   Well, come, my Kate, we will unto your father's
170   Even in these honest mean habiliments;
Our purses shall be proud, our garments poor,
For 'tis the mind that makes the body rich;
And as the sun breaks through the darkest clouds,
So honor peereth in the meanest habit.
175   What, is the jay more precious than the lark,
Because his fathers are more beautiful?
Or is the adder better than the eel,
Because his painted skin contents the eye?
O, no, good Kate; neither art thou the worse
180   For this poor furniture and mean array.
If thou accountedst it shame, lay it on me,
And therefore frolic, we will hence forthwith,
To feast and sport us at thy father's house.
Go call my men, and let us straight to him,
185   And bring our horses unto Long-lane end;
There will we mount, and thither walk on foot.
Let's see, I think 'tis now some seven a'clock,
And well we may come there by dinner-time.

Katherina   I dare assure you, sir, 'tis almost two,
190   And 'twill be supper-time ere you come there.

Petruchio   It shall be seven ere I go to horse.
Look what I speak, or do, or think to do,
You are still crossing it. Sirs, let't alone,
I will not go to-day, and ere I do,
195   It shall be what a'clock I say it is.

Hortensio   [*Aside.*] Why, so this gallant will command
the sun.

[*Exeunt.*]

Petruchio   Well, come along, my Kate, we will go to your father's house in just these plain, respectable clothes. Our finances shall be strong though our garments be humble, for it is the mind that truly adorns the body. Just as the sun breaks through the darkest clouds, honor is easily seen even when one wears the most ordinary outfit. Is the blue jay of more value than the lark because his feathers are more beautiful? Is the adder better than the eel because his patterned skin is more attractive to the eye? Oh, no, good Kate, and you are no less valuable because you wear a plain gown with no ornamentation. If you consider it shameful, blame it on me. Therefore, cheer up. We will leave soon to feast and celebrate at your father's house.

[*to* **Grumio**] Go, call my servants and let's go directly there. Bring our horses to the end of Long Lane. We'll walk that far on foot and mount our horses there. Let's see. I think it's now about seven o'clock, and we can easily arrive there in time for the midday dinner.

Katherina   I do assure you, sir, it's almost two and it will be suppertime before we arrive.

Petruchio   [*in exasperation*] It will be seven before I mount my horse. No matter what I say or do or think, you are still contradicting it!

[*to* **Servants**] Men, never mind. I won't go today, and when I do go, it shall be whatever time I say it is.

Hortensio   [*to himself*] Well, so this fellow will even tell the sun what to do.

[*They all leave.*]

Scene 4

Enter **Tranio** [*as Lucentio*], *and* the **Pedant** *dress'd like Vincentio,* [*booted and bare-headed*].

Tranio   [Sir], this is the house, please it you that I call?

Pedant   Ay, what else? And but I be deceived,
Signior Baptista may remember me
Near twenty years ago in Genoa,
5 Where we were lodgers at the Pegasus.

Tranio   'Tis well, and hold your own in any case
With such austerity as 'longeth to a father.

Enter **Biondello**

Pedant   I warrant you. But, sir, here comes your boy;
'Twere good he were school'd.

10 **Tranio**   Fear you not him. Sirrah Biondello,
Now do your duty throughly, I advise you.
Imagine 'twere the right Vincentio.

Biondello   Tut, fear not me.

Tranio   But hast thou done thy errand to Baptista?

Biondello   I told him that your father was at Venice,
16 And that you look'd for him this day in Padua.

Scene 4

*In front of **Baptista's** house. [**Tranio**, disguised as **Lucentio**, and the **Pedant**, as **Vincentio**, enter.]*

Tranio   Sir, this is the house. Would you like me to knock?

Pedant   Yes, of course. Unless I am mistaken, Signior Baptista may remember me from about twenty years ago when we were both staying in Genoa at the Pegasus Inn.

Tranio   Don't worry. Just maintain your role with all the dignity appropriate to a father, no matter what happens.

Pedant   I will do so.

[**Biondello** *enters.*]

But, sir, here comes your servant. It would be a good idea to coach him on what's happening.

Tranio   Don't worry about him.

[*to* **Biondello**] Now, Biondello, my lad, I order you to fully perform your duties; just pretend that this is the real Vincentio.

Biondello   Oh, don't worry about me.

Tranio   But have you performed your errand to Baptista?

Biondello   [*nodding vigorously*] I told him that your father was in Venice and that you expected him to arrive in Padua today.

Tranio   Th' art a tall fellow; hold thee that to drink.
Here comes Baptista; set your countenance, sir.

Enter **Baptista** *and* **Lucentio** [*as Cambio*].

Signior Baptista, you are happily met.

20   [*To the Pedant.*] Sir, this is the gentleman I told you of.
I pray you stand good father to me now,
Give me Bianca for my patrimony.

Pedant   Soft son!
Sir, by your leave, having come to Padua
25   To gather in some debts, my son Lucentio
Made me acquainted with a weighty cause
Of love between your daughter and himself;
And for the good report I hear of you,
And for the love he beareth to your daughter,
30   And she to him, to stay him not too long,
I am content, in a good father's care,
To have him match'd; and if you please to like
No worse than I, upon some agreement
Me shall you find ready and willing
35   With one consent to have her so bestowed;
For curious I cannot be with you,
Signior Baptista, of whom I hear so well.

Tranio   [*tossing him a coin*] You're a fine fellow. Keep that to buy yourself a drink with.

[*softly, to the* **Pedant**] Here comes Baptista. Put on your dignified expression, sir.

[**Baptista** *enters with* **Lucentio**, *disguised as* **Cambio**.]

[*to* **Baptista**] Signior Baptista, how nice to see you!

[*to the* **Pedant** *as if to* **Vincentio**] Sir, this is the gentleman I told you about. I ask you to be a good father to me now. Give me Bianca for my inheritance.

Pedant   [*speaking as* **Vincentio**] Easy, son!

[*to* **Baptista**] Sir, if I may speak. I have come to Padua to collect some debts, and my son Lucentio has informed me of a serious matter, that is, the love between my daughter and him. Because of your good reputation and because of the love he has for your daughter and she has for him, I will not make him wait. I am content, as his loving father, to permit him to marry, and, upon the legal terms being settled, if you have no objections you shall find that I am ready and willing to be united with you in giving our consent to give her to him. I have no desire to haggle with you, Signior Baptista, having heard so many good things about you.

Bapista   Sir, pardon me in what I have to say—
Your plainness and your shortness please me well.
40 Right true it is, your son Lucentio here
Doth love my daughter, and she loveth him,
Or both dissemble deeply their affections;
And therefore if you say no more than this,
That like a father you will deal with him,
45 And pass my daughter a sufficient dower,
The match is made, and all is done:
Your son shall have my daughter with consent.

Tranio   I thank you, sir. Where then do you know best
We be affied and such assurance ta'en
50 As shall with either part's agreement stand?

Bapista   Not in my house, Lucentio, for you know
Pitchers have ears, and I have many servants;
Besides, old Gremio is heark'ning still,
And happily we might be interrupted.

55 **Tranio**   Then at my lodging, and it like you.
There doth my father lie; and there this night
We'll pass the business privately and well.
Send for your daughter by your servant here;
My boy shall fetch the scrivener presently.
60 The worst is this, that at so slender warning,
You are like to have a thin and slender pittance.

Bapista   It likes me well. Cambio, hie you home,
And bid Bianca make her ready straight;
And if you will, tell what hath happened:
65 Lucentio's father is arriv'd in Padua,
And how she's like to be Lucentio's wife.

[Exit Lucentio.]

Baptista   Sir, don't be offended by what I have to say. I like your straightforwardness and brevity. It's quite true that your son Lucentio here loves my daughter, and she loves him—or both of them are completely faking their feelings. [*He chuckles at his witticism.*] And therefore, if you will give me your word that you will deal with him as if you were his father and if you will give my daughter a sufficient dowry, the match is made and everything is settled. Your son shall have my permission to have my daughter.

Tranio   [*speaking as* **Lucentio**] Thank you, sir! [*He shakes* **Baptista's** *hand and then, pretending to be swept away by delight, hugs him.*] Where do you prefer that we finalize the engagement and draw up the documents that will settle both parties' rights in the agreement?

Baptista   Not at my house, Lucentio, for, as you know, even pitchers have "ears," and I have many servants. Besides, old Gremio is still snooping around, and we might be interrupted. [**Baptista** *refers to the handles of pitchers which are shaped somewhat like ears. He means that those who have servants must always be on guard against being overheard by them.*]

Tranio   Then at the place where I am staying, if that's all right with you. My father also is staying there, and tonight we may complete this business privately and fully. Send this servant of yours for your daughter; my servant shall fetch the notary right away. The worst of it is that, with such short notice, you are likely to have a skimpy meal provided.

Baptista   I am fine with that.

[*to* **Lucentio** *as* **Cambio**] Cambio, hurry home and tell Bianca to get ready right away, and, if you like, tell her what has happened: that Lucentio's father has arrived in Padua and that she is likely to become Lucentio's wife. [**Lucentio** *leaves.*]

Biondello   I pray the gods she may with all my heart!

Tranio   Dally not with the gods, but get thee gone.

Exit [Biondello].

*Enter **Peter**, [a servant, who whispers to Tranio].*

Signior Baptista, shall I lead the way?
70   Welcome! one mess is like to be your cheer.
Come, sir, we will better it in Pisa.

Bapista   I follow you.

Exeunt.

*Enter **Lucentio** [as Cambio] and **Biondello**.*

Biondello   Cambio!

Lucentio   What say'st thou, Biondello?

Biondello   You saw my master wink and laugh upon
76   you?

Lucentio   Biondello, what of that?

Biondello   Faith, nothing; but h'as left me here behind
to expound the meaning or moral of his signs and
80   tokens.

Lucentio   I pray thee moralize them.

Biondello   Then thus; Baptista is safe, talking with the
deceiving father of a deceitful son.

Lucentio   And what of him?

Biondello   His daughter is to be brought by you to
86   the supper.

Biondello   I pray that she may with all my heart!

Tranio   [*to* **Biondello**] Don't take time to pray. Just get going.

[**Biondello** *leaves.* **Peter**, *a servant, enters and whispers to* **Tranio**.]

[*speaking as* **Lucentio**] Signior Baptista, shall I lead the way to my lodgings? You are welcome there. You will probably only get one course to eat, but we'll feed you better when you come to Pisa, sir.

Baptista   I'll follow you.

[**Tranio**, *as* **Lucentio**; *the* **Pedant**, *as* **Vincentio**; *and* **Baptista** *leave together.*]

[**Lucentio**, *as* **Cambio**, *and* **Biondello** *return.*]

Biondello   Cambio!

Lucentio   What is it, Biondello?

Biondello   Did you see my master wink and laugh at you?

Lucentio   What of it, Biondello?

Biondello   Nothing really, but he has left me behind to explain the meaning of his signs and signals.

Lucentio   Then please explain them.

Biondello   Just this. Baptista is out of the way, talking with the fake father of a fake son.

Lucentio   Go on.

Biondello   His daughter is to be brought by you to the supper.

Lucentio   And then?

Biondello   The old priest of Saint Luke's church is at
your command at all hours.

90 **Lucentio**   And what of all this?

Biondello   I cannot tell, [expect] they are busied
about a counterfeit assurance. Take you assurance
of her, *cum privilegio ad imprimendum solum*; to th'
church take the priest, clerk, and some sufficient
95   honest witnesses.
If this be not that you look for, I have no more to say,
But bid Bianca farewell for ever and a day.

Lucentio   Hear'st thou, Biondello?

Biondello   I cannot tarry. I knew a wench married
100   in an afternoon as she went to the garden for
parsley to stuff a rabbit, and so may you, sir: And so
adieu, sir; my master hath appointed me to go to
Saint Luke's to bid the priest be ready to come against
you come with your appendix.

Exit.

105 **Lucentio**   I may and will, if she be so contented.
She will be pleas'd, then wherefore should I doubt?
Hap what hap may, I'll roundly go about her;
It shall go hard if Cambio go without her.

Exit.

Lucentio   [*His eyes sparkle as he grasps the plan.*] And then?

Biondello   The old priest of St. Luke's church is available whenever you want him.

Lucentio   [*pretending that he hasn't caught* **Biondello's** *drift yet*] And what does it all mean?

Biondello   I have no idea, except that they are busy drawing up false papers, and while they do that, you may take her and stake your claim to her. Go to the church, take the priest, the clerk, and some reasonably honest witnesses. If this isn't what you had hoped for, I have nothing else to say except that you should just say goodbye to Bianca forever.

[**Biondello** *starts to leave.*]

Lucentio   Hey, Biondello!

Biondello   I can't wait. I knew a girl who was married one afternoon when she went to the garden to get parsley to stuff a rabbit. And you may marry just as quickly, sir. So goodbye, sir. My master has ordered me to go to St. Luke's to tell the priest to be ready in case you should show up with your bride.

[**Biondello** *leaves.*]

Lucentio   I may. [*He is shaken by a passing doubt.*] I will do so if she is willing. [*He attempts to reassure himself.*] She will be happy about it. So why should I be worried? Let happen what will happen, I'll go straight there to marry her. [*His doubts return.*] It will be bad if she won't come with "Cambio."

[**Lucentio** *leaves.*]

Scene 5

Enter **Petruchio**, **Kate**, **Hortensio**, [*and* **Servants**].

Petruchio   Come on, a' God's name, once more toward
    our father's.
Good Lord, how bright and goodly shines the moon!

Katherina   The moon! the sun—it is not moonlight now.

Petruchio   I say it is the moon that shines so bright.

Katherina   I know it is the sun that shines so bright.

6 **Petruchio**   Now, by my mother's son, and that's myself,
It shall be moon, or star, or what I list,
Or ere I journey to your father's house.—
Go on, and fetch our horses back again.—
10 Evermore cross'd and cross'd, nothing but cross'd!

Hortensio   Say as he says, or we shall never go.

Katherina   Forward, I pray, since we have come so far,
And be it moon, or sun, or what you please;
An if you please to call it a rush-candle,
15 Henceforth I vow it shall be so for me.

Petruchio   I say it is the moon.

Katherina   I know it is the moon.

Petruchio   Nay, then you lie; it is the blessed sun.

Scene 5

A public road.

[**Petruchio**, **Katherina**, **Hortensio**, *and* **Servants** *enter, on horseback.*]

Petruchio   Come on, by God, we head once more to your father Baptista's house. [*He looks up at the sky.*] Good Lord, the moon shines bright and strong!

Katherina   [*thinking he has misspoken*] The moon! It's the sun. There is no moonlight now.

Petruchio   I say it is the moon that shines so brightly.

Katherina   I know it is the *sun* that shines so brightly.

Petruchio   Now, I swear by my mother's son, and I am he, it shall be the moon or a star or whatever I choose before I will journey to your father's house.

[*to* **Servants**] Go on and bring our pack horses back again.

[*to himself*] Always contradicted and contradicted, nothing but contradicted!

Hortensio   [*softly, to* **Katherina**] Agree with him or we'll never go.

Katherina   [*swallowing hard at having to agree with* **Petruchio**] Let's go on, please, since we've come so far. It will be the moon or the sun or whatever you wish, and if you prefer to call it a cheap little candle, I promise you that from now on it will be just that for me.

Petruchio   [*testing her*] I say it is the moon.

Katherina   [*agreeing serenely*] I *know* it is the moon.

Petruchio   Then you lie! It is the blessed sun.

Katherina   Then God be blest, it [is] the blessed sun,
But sun it is not, when you say it is not;
20   And the moon changes even as your mind.
What you will have it nam'd, even that it is,
And so it shall be so for Katherine.

Hortensio   Petruchio, go thy ways, the field is won.

Petruchio   Well, forward, forward, thus the bowl should run,
25   And not unluckily against the bias.
But soft, company is coming here.

Enter **Vincentio**.

[*To Vincentio.*]
Good morrow, gentle mistress, where away?
Tell me, sweet Kate, and tell me truly too,
Hast thou beheld a fresher gentlewoman?
30   Such war of white and red within her cheeks!
What stars do spangle heaven with such beauty,
As those two eyes become that heavenly face?
Fair lovely maid, once more good day to thee.
Sweet Kate, embrace her for her beauty's sake.

Hortensio   'A will make the man mad, to make [a]
36   woman of him.

Katherina   Young budding virgin, fair, and fresh, and sweet,
Whither away, or [where] is thy abode?
Happy the parents of so fair a child!
40   Happier the man whom favorable stars
Allots thee for his lovely bedfellow!

Katherina   Then, bless God, it *is* the blessed sun. But when you say it isn't the sun, then it isn't, and the moon changes as often as you change your mind. Whatever you want to call it, that's what it is, and that is how it shall be for me.

Hortensio   [*softly, to* **Petruchio**] Petruchio, it's over. You've won the war.

Petruchio   Well, let's go, let's go! That's the way the ball goes when it rolls straight and not off its course. But, wait! Someone is coming.

[**Vincentio** *enters.*]

[*to* **Vincentio**] Good day, dear lady. Where are you headed?

[*to* **Katherina**] Tell me, sweet Kate, and be truthful, too— Have you ever seen a gentlewoman with such a healthy glow? Such a fresh flush of color is in her cheeks! The stars don't adorn the sky with such beauty as those two eyes adorn that heavenly face! Most lovely maiden, once more I say good day to you. Sweet Kate, embrace her for how beautiful she is. [*As* **Petruchio** *speaks,* **Vincentio** *looks around in comic confusion.*]

Hortensio   [*to himself*] It will drive the man insane to be turned into a woman.

Katherina   [*speaking with elaborate courtesy, to* **Vincentio's** *increasing mystification*] Young blooming virgin, lovely and fresh and sweet, where are you going? Or where is your home? How happy are the parents of such a lovely child! And even happier is the man who is fortunate enough to have you as the lovely woman with whom he shares his bed.

Petruchio   Why, how now, Kate, I hope thou art not mad.
This is a man, old, wrinkled, faded, withered,
And not a maiden, as thou say'st he is.

45 **Katherina**   Pardon, old father, my mistaking eyes,
That have been so bedazzled with the sun,
That every thing I look on seemeth green;
Now I perceive thou art a reverent father.
Pardon, I pray thee, for my mad mistaking.

50 **Petruchio**   Do, good old grandsire, and withal make known
Which way thou travellest—if along with us,
We shall be joyful of thy company.

Vincentio   Fair sir, and you my merry mistress,
That with your strange encounter much amaz'd me,
55 My name is call'd Vincentio, my dwelling Pisa,
And bound I am to Padua, there to visit
A son of mine, which long I have not seen.

Petruchio   What is his name?

Vincentio   Lucentio, gentle sir.

Petruchio   Happily met, the happier for thy son.
60 And now by law, as well as reverent age,
I may entitle thee my loving father.
The sister to my wife, this gentlewoman,
Thy son by this hath married. Wonder not,
Nor be grieved; she is of good esteem,
65 Her dowry wealthy, and of worthy birth;
Beside, so qualified as may beseem
The spouse of any noble gentleman.
Let me embrace with old Vincentio,
And wander we to see thy honest son,
70 Who will of thy arrival be full joyous.

Petruchio   Why, what are you saying, Kate? I hope you haven't lost your mind! This is a wrinkled, faded, withered old man and not a young maiden as you say he is.

Katherina   Old father, forgive my blundering eyes. The sun is so bright that everything I look at seems to be youthful. I now see that you are a respectable old man. Please forgive my crazy error.

Petruchio   Please do, good old grandfather. Tell us which way you are headed. If you are going the same way we are, we would be happy to have your company.

Vincentio   Dear sir and my jolly mistress, you have truly amazed me with the strange way you greeted me. My name is Vincentio. I live in Pisa and I'm headed to Padua to visit my son, whom I haven't seen in a long time.

Petruchio   What is his name?

Vincentio   Lucentio, sir.

Petruchio   How fortunate that we've met, and even more fortunate for your son. Both the law and your own seniority allow me to call you my loving "father." Your son has married the sister of my wife, this lady here. Don't be amazed or saddened. She is a woman of good reputation, with a very large dowry and of excellent social rank. Furthermore, she has all the qualities that the wife of any nobleman should have. Let me embrace you, old Vincentio, and let's travel to see your honest son who will be delighted at your arrival.

Vincentio   But is this true, or is it else your pleasure,
Like pleasant travellers, to break a jest
Upon the company you overtake?

Hortensio   I do assure thee, father, so it is.

75 **Petruchio**   Come go along and see the truth hereof,
For our first merriment hath made thee jealous.

Exeunt [all but Hortensio].

Hortensio   Well, Petruchio, this has put me in heart.
Have to my widow! and if she [be] froward,
Then hast thou taught Hortensio to be untoward.

Exit.

Vincentio   Is this really true? Or have you decided to amuse yourselves like cheerful travelers do, to put over a joke on those you happen to meet on your journey?

Hortensio   I assure you, father, that it's true.

Petruchio   Come, let's go and you will see the truth of the matter, for our earlier joking has made you suspicious.

[*All but* **Hortensio** *leave.*]

Hortensio   [*speaking to himself*] Well, Petruchio, this has encouraged me. Look out, widow! If she is headstrong, then you, Petruchio, have taught me to be outrageous.

[**Hortensio** *leaves.*]

Act five

Scene 1

Enter **Biondello, Lucentio,** *and* **Bianca; Gremio** *is out before.*

Biondello   Softly and swiftly, sir, for the priest is ready.

Lucentio   I fly, Biondello; but they may chance to need
thee at home, therefore leave us.

Biondello   Nay, faith, I'll see the church a' your back,
5   and then come back to my [master's] as soon
as I can.

[*Exeunt Lucentio, Bianca, and Biondello.*]

Gremio   I marvel Cambio comes not all this while.

Enter **Petruchio, Kate, Vincentio, Grumio,** *with* **Attendants**.

Petruchio   Sir, here's the door, this is Lucentio's house.
My father's bears more toward the market-place;
10   Thither must I, and here I leave you, sir.

Vincentio   You shall not choose but drink before you go.
I think I shall command your welcome here;
And by all likelihood some cheer is toward.

Knock.

Act five

Scene 1

In front of **Lucentio's** *house in Padua.*

[**Biondello**, **Lucentio**, and **Bianca** *enter.* **Gremio**, *already present, is snooping around* **Lucentio's** *house.*]

Biondello   We must be quiet and quick, sir, for the priest is ready.

Lucentio   I'm hurrying, Biondello. But they may need you at home, so leave us.

Biondello   No, indeed, I'll see you to the church and then go back to my master's as soon as I can.

[**Biondello**, **Lucentio**, and **Bianca** *leave.*]

Gremio   [*not having seen* **Biondello**, **Lucentio**, *and* **Bianca**] I'm surprised that Cambio hasn't come in all this time.

[**Petruchio**, **Katherina**, **Vincentio**, *and* **Servants** *enter.*]

Petruchio   Sir, here is the door. This is Lucentio's house. My father-in-law's is nearer to the marketplace. I must go there, so I must leave you here, sir.

Vincentio   I'm sure that you must want a drink before you go. I shall give orders that you be welcomed here, and, in all likelihood, some sort of feast is being prepared to welcome me.

[**Vincentio** *knocks at the door but receives no answer.*]

233

Gremio   They're busy within, you were best knock
15   louder.

> **Pendant** *looks out of the window.*

Pedant   What's he that knocks as he would beat
down the gate?

Vincentio   Is Signior Lucentio within, sir?

Pedant   He's within, sir, but not to be spoken
20   withal.

Vincentio   What if a man bring him a hundred pound
or two, to make merry withal?

Pedant   Keep your hundred pounds to yourself, he
24   shall need none so long as I live.

Petruchio   Nay, I told you your son was well belov'd
in Padua. Do you hear, sir?—to leave frivolous
circumstances, I pray you tell Signior Lucentio that
his father is come from Pisa, and is here at the door
29   to speak with him.

Pedant   Thou liest, his father is come from Padua
and here looking out at the window.

Vincentio   Art thou his father?

Pedant   Ay, sir, so his mother says, if I may believe
34   her.

Petruchio   [*To Vincentio.*] Why, how now, gentleman?
Why, this is flat knavery, to take upon you another
man's name.

Gremio   [*stepping forward to comment*] They're busy in there. You'd better knock more loudly.

[*The **Pedant**, masquerading as **Vincentio**, looks out an upper window.*]

Pedant   [*impatiently*] Who is knocking as if he intends to knock down the door?

Vincentio   Is Signior Lucentio at home, sir?

Pedant   He is, sir, but he can't be interrupted.

Vincentio   [*amused at being denied entry to his son's house*] What if a man were to bring him one or two hundred pounds to enjoy himself with? [*The pound is a unit of British currency.*]

Pedant   You may keep your one hundred pounds to yourself. He won't need them as long as I'm alive.

Petruchio   [*to **Vincentio***] I told you your son was well liked in Padua. Do you hear that, sir?

[*to **Pedant***] Setting aside unimportant matters, sir, please tell Signior Lucentio that his father has arrived from Pisa and is here at the door to speak with him.

Pedant   [*starting in dismay but trying to bluff his way out*] You lie! His father is here from Padua, and he is looking out the window at you. [*The **Pedant** refers to himself in the third person.*]

Vincentio   [*unable to believe his ears*] Are you his father?

Pedant   Yes, sir, at least that's what his mother says, if I may believe her. [*He smirks at the old witticism.*]

Petruchio   [*to the real **Vincentio***] Why, what's this, sir? Why, this is villainy, to use another man's name as if it were your own!

Pedant   Lay hands on the villain. I believe 'a means
to cozen somebody in this city under my coun-
40   tenance.

Enter **Biondello**.

Biondello   I have seen them in the church together,
God send 'em good shipping! But who is here?
Mine old master Vincentio! Now we are undone
and brought to nothing.

Vincentio   [*Seeing Biondello.*]
46   Come hither, crack-hemp.

Biondello   I hope I may choose, sir.

Vincentio   Come hither, you rogue. What, have you
forgot me?

Biondello   Forgot you? no, sir. I could not forget
51   you, for I never saw you before in all my life.

Vincentio   What, you notorious villain, didst thou
never see thy [master's] father, Vincentio?

Biondello   What, my old worshipful old master?
Yes, marry, sir—see where he looks out of the
56   window.

Vincentio   Is't so, indeed?

He beats Biondello.

Biondello   Help, help, help! here's a madman will
murder me.

[*Exit.*]

60 **Pedant**   Help, son! help, Signior Baptista!

[*Exit above.*]

Pedant   [*in great indignation*] Arrest the scoundrel! I believe he intends to cheat someone in this city by pretending to be me.

[**Biondello** *enters.*]

Biondello   [*to himself*] I've seen them get married in the church. God bless their lives together. But who is here? My old master Vincentio! Now we're in deep trouble and everything is ruined!

Vincentio   [*Catching sight of* **Biondello** *as he's about to slink away unseen,* **Vincentio** *calls to him.*] Come here, you crook!

Biondello   [*pretending not to know* **Vincentio**] I hope I have a choice about it, sir.

Vincentio   [*roaring*] Come here, you scoundrel! What, have you forgotten who I am?

Biondello   Forgotten you! No, sir, I couldn't forget you because I've never seen you before in my life.

Vincentio   Why, you infamous villain, you say you've never seen your master's father, Vincentio?

Biondello   [*desperately stalling for time*] What, my old honorable old master? Yes, indeed, sir. There he is looking out the window. [*He points to the* **Pedant**.]

Vincentio: [*threateningly*] Is that so? [*He beats* **Biondello**.]

Biondello   Help! Help! This madman is trying to murder me!

[**Biondello** *runs off.*]

Pedant   [*Still pretending to be* **Vincentio**, *he calls to those within the house.*] Help, son! Help, Signior Baptista!

[*The* **Pedant** *pulls his head back into the house.*]

Petruchio Prithee, Kate, let's stand aside and see the
end of this controversy.

[They retire.]

Enter **Pedant** [below] *with* **Servants**, **Baptista**, **Tranio**
[*as* Lucentio].

64 **Tranio** Sir, what are you that offer to beat my servant?

Vincentio What am I, sir? Nay, what are you, sir?
O immortal gods! O fine villain! A silken doublet,
a velvet hose, a scarlet cloak, and a copatain hat!
O, I am undone, I am undone! While I play the good
husband at home, my son and my servant spend all
70 at the university.

Tranio How now, what's the matter?

Baptista What, is the man lunatic?

Tranio Sir, you seem a sober ancient gentleman by
your habit; but your words show you a madman.
75 Why, sir, what 'cerns it you if I wear pearl and
gold? I thank my good father, I am able to maintain it.

Vincentio Thy father! O villain, he is a sailmaker in
Bergamo.

Baptista You mistake, sir, you mistake, sir. Pray,
80 what do you think is his name?

Vincentio His name! as if I knew not his name! I
have brought him up ever since he was three years
old, and his name is Tranio.

Petruchio   What do you say, Kate? Let's watch from over here and see how this quarrel ends.

[*They stand off to one side.*]

[*The* **Pedant,** *as* **Vincentio**; **Tranio,** *as* **Lucentio**; **Baptista,** *and* **Servants** *come out of the house.*]

Tranio   [*speaking as* **Lucentio**] Sir, who do you think you are, that you beat my servant?

Vincentio   [*beside himself at hearing his own servant address him in such a way*] Who am I, sir? No, who are you, sir? Oh, immortal gods! Oh, you complete villain! Wearing a silk jacket, velvet trousers, a scarlet cloak, and a fashionable hat! Oh, I am ruined! I am ruined! While I work hard to earn money at home, my son and his servant spend it all at the university. [**Vincentio** *assumes that* **Lucentio** *has squandered money by buying ridiculously expensive clothing for his servant,* **Tranio.**]

Tranio   [*still as* **Lucentio**] What? What's the matter?

Baptista   [*to* **Tranio/Lucentio**] What, is this man insane?

Tranio   Sir, by the way you are dressed you seem to be a respectable older gentleman, but you talk like a lunatic. Why, sir, what concern is it of yours if I wear pearls and gold? Thanks to my good father, I can afford to do so.

Vincentio   Your father! You scoundrel! Your father is a sailmaker in Bergamo.

Baptista   You are wrong, sir, you are wrong. Tell me, what do you think his name is?

Vincentio   His name! As if I didn't know his name! I've raised him ever since he was three years old. His name is Tranio. [**Tranio,** *continuing the masquerade, shrugs, pretends to be mystified at being mistaken for someone else.*]

Pedant   Away, away, mad ass, his name is Lucentio,
and he is mine only son, and heir to the lands of me,
86   Signior Vincentio.

Vincentio   Lucentio! O, he hath murd'red his master!
Lay hold on him, I charge you, in the Duke's name.
O, my son, my son! Tell me, thou villain, where is
90   my son Lucentio?

Tranio   Call forth an officer.

[*Exit Servant, who returns with an Officer.*]

Carry this mad knave to the jail. Father Baptista,
I charge you see that he be forthcoming.

Vincentio   Carry me to the jail?

95 **Gremio**   Stay, officer, he shall not go to prison.

Baptista   Talk not, Signior Gremio; I say he shall go
to prison.

Gremio   Take heed, Signior Baptista, lest you be
cony-catch'd in this business. I dare swear this is the
100   right Vincentio.

Pedant   Swear, if thou dar'st.

Gremio   Nay, I dare not swear it.

Tranio   Then thou wert best say that I am not
104   Lucentio.

Gremio   Yes, I know thee to be Signior Lucentio.

Pedant   Go on! Get out of here, you crazy ass! His name is Lucentio, and he is my only son and heir to the property belonging to me, Signior Vincentio.

Vincentio   [*Believing he at last understands what is going on, he points accusingly at* **Tranio**.] Lucentio! Oh, he has murdered his master! Arrest him, I order you, in the name of the duke. [*clutching his head in despair*] Oh, my son, my son! Tell me, you villain, where is my son, Lucentio?

Tranio   Get a police officer!

[*Someone enters with an officer.*]

[*to* **Officer**] Take this mad scoundrel to the jail.

[*to* **Baptista**] Father Baptista, I ask you to see that he is safely locked up.

Vincentio   Lock *me* up?

Gremio   [**Gremio** *steps out of hiding.*] Wait, officer! Don't take him to prison.

Baptista   Be silent, Signior Gremio. I say he shall go to prison.

Gremio   Be careful, Signior Baptista, that you don't wind up being swindled in this business. I would swear this is the real Vincentio. [*He points to the real* **Vincentio** *as he speaks.*]

Pedant   [*bluffing, with false haughtiness*] Swear it, if you dare.

Gremio   Well, no, I wouldn't actually *swear* to it.

Tranio   You might as well claim that I am not Lucentio.

Gremio   No, I know that you are Signior Lucentio.

Baptista   Away with the dotard, to the jail with him!

Enter **Biondello**, **Lucentio**, *and* **Bianca**.

Vincentio   Thus strangers may be hal'd and abus'd. O
109   monstrous villain!

Biondello   O, we are spoil'd and—yonder he is. Deny
him, forswear him, or else we are all undone.

Exeunt Biondello, Tranio, and Pedant, as fast as may be.

Lucentio   Pardon, sweet father.

Kneel.

Vincentio   Lives my sweet son?

Bianca   Pardon, dear father.

Baptista   How hast thou offended?
Where is Lucentio?

Lucentio   Here's Lucentio,
115   Right son to the right Vincentio,
That have by marriage made thy daughter mine,
While counterfeit supposes blear'd thine eyne.

Gremio   Here's packing, with a witness, to deceive us
all!

Baptista   [*impatiently*] Take the senile old fool away! Take him to jail!

Vincentio   [*struggling in the officer's grasp*] So this is how you treat strangers? First you welcome them and then you abuse them!

[*to* **Tranio**] Oh, you wicked scoundrel!

[**Biondello** *returns with the blissful couple,* **Lucentio** *and* **Bianca**. *He stops short, deeply dismayed at seeing the assembled crowd.*]

Biondello   Oh, no! We're in trouble and—!

[*to* **Lucentio**, *referring to the real* **Vincentio**] There he is! Deny that you know him! Denounce him, or else we're all in hot water!

Lucentio   [*kneeling before his father*] Forgive me, my dear father.

Vincentio   [*overcome with relief and joy*] Is my beloved son alive? [*Father and son embrace.*]

[**Biondello**, **Tranio**, *and the* **Pedant** *scurry away while everyone watches* **Vincentio** *and* **Lucentio**.]

Bianca   [*kneeling to* **Baptista**] Forgive me, dear father.

Baptista   [*thoroughly confused*] What have you done wrong? [*looking for the false* **Lucentio**] Which is Lucentio?

Lucentio   I am Lucentio, the real son to the real Vincentio. [*He gestures toward his father.*] I have made your daughter mine by marriage while the false "father" and "son" deceived your eyes.

Gremio   [*indignantly*] Undoubtedly this has all been plotted to hoodwink us!

120 **Vincentio**   Where is that damned villain Tranio,
That fac'd and braved me in this matter so?

Baptista   Why, tell me, is not this my Cambio?

Biondello   Cambio is chang'd into Lucentio.

Lucentio   Love wrought these miracles. Bianca's love
125 Made me exchange my state with Tranio,
While he did bear my countenance in the town,
And happily I have arrived at the last
Unto the wished haven of my bliss.
What Tranio did, myself enforc'd him to;
130 Then pardon him, sweet father, for my sake.

Vincentio   I'll slit the villain's nose, that would have
sent me to the jail.

Baptista   But do you hear, sir? Have you married my
daughter without asking my good will?

Vincentio   Fear not, Baptista, we will content you, go
136 to; but I will in to be reveng'd for this villany.

Exit.

Baptista   And I, to sound the depth of this knavery.

Exit.

Lucentio   Look not pale, Bianca, thy father will not
frown.

Exeunt [Lucentio and Bianca].

Vincentio   [*looking around for one of the culprits*] Where is that damned villain Tranio who stood up to me and defied me as he did?

Baptista   Do you mean to tell me that this is not Cambio? [*He points to* **Lucentio**.]

Bianca   [*smiling up at* **Lucentio**] Cambio is transformed into Lucentio.

Lucentio   Love has performed these miracles. In order to win Bianca's love, I changed places with Tranio while he pretended to be me here in town. And I have finally reached the heavenly haven I was hoping to reach. What Tranio did, he did at my command, so forgive him, dear Father, for my sake.

Vincentio   I'll slit the scoundrel's nose! He would have sent me to prison.

Baptista   [*to* **Vincentio**] But do you hear that, sir?

[*indignantly, to* **Lucentio**] Have you really married my daughter without my consent?

Vincentio   Don't worry, Baptista. I will make sure you are satisfied. But I'm going inside to see to it that this treachery is avenged.

[**Vincentio** *leaves.*]

Baptista   And I, too, will get to the bottom of this treachery.

[**Baptista** *leaves.*]

Lucentio   Don't look so frightened, Bianca. Your father won't be angry at you.

[**Lucentio** *and* **Bianca** *leave.*]

Gremio   My cake is dough, but I'll in among the
140   rest,
　　　Out of hope of all but my share of the feast.

　　　　　　　　　　　　　　　　　　　　　　[*Exit.*]

Katherina   Husband, let's follow, to see the end of
　　　this ado.

Petruchio   First kiss me, Kate, and we will.

Katherina   What, in the midst of the street?

145 **Petruchio**   What, art thou asham'd of me?

Katherina   No, sir, God forbid, but asham'd to kiss.

Petruchio   Why then let's home again. Come, sirrah,
　　　let's away.

Katherina   Nay, I will give thee a kiss; now pray thee,
　　　love, stay.

149 **Petruchio**   Is not this well? Come, my sweet Kate:
　　　Better once than never, for never too late.

　　　　　　　　　　　　　　　　　　　　　　Exeunt.

Gremio   My plans are all ruined, but I'll go in with the rest of them. I have no hope left except that I might get a share of the wedding feast.

[**Gremio** *leaves, shaking his head.*]

Katherina   Husband, let's follow them to see what comes of all this.

Petruchio   First kiss me, Kate, and we will.

Katherina   What, in the middle of the street?

Petruchio   Why? Are you ashamed of me?

Katherina   No, sir, God forbid! Just ashamed to kiss in public.

Petruchio   Why, then let's go home again.

[*to* **Grumio**] Come, fellow, let's go.

Katherina   No, wait! I will give you a kiss. [*She kisses* **Petruchio**.] Now, please, darling, stay.

Petruchio   Isn't this good? Come, my sweet Kate. Better late than never because it's never too late.

[**Petruchio** *and* **Katherina** *leave.*]

Scene 2

Enter **Baptista**, **Vincentio**, **Gremio**, *the* **Pedant**, **Lucentio**, *and* **Bianca**; [**Petruchio**, **Katherina**, **Hortensio**,] **Tranio**, **Biondello**, **Grumio**, *and* **Widow**: *the servingmen with Tranio bringing in a banquet.*

Lucentio At last, though long, our jarring notes agree,
And time it is, when raging war is [done],
To smile at scapes and perils overblown.
My fair Bianca, bid my father welcome,
5   While I with self-same kindness welcome thine.
Brother Petruchio, sister Katherina,
And thou, Hortensio, with thy loving widow,
Feast with the best, and welcome to my house.
My banket is to close our stomachs up
10   After our great good cheer. Pray you sit down,
For now we sit to chat as well as eat.

Petruchio Nothing but sit and sit, and eat and eat!

Baptista Padua affords this kindness, son Petruchio.

Petruchio Padua affords nothing but what is kind.

Hortensio For both our sakes, I would that word were
15   true.

Petruchio Now, for my life, Hortensio fears his widow.

Widow Then never trust me if I be afeard.

Petruchio You are very sensible, and yet you miss my
sense:
I mean Hortensio is afeard of you.

Scene 2

Inside **Lucentio's** *house in Padua.*

[**Baptista, Vincentio, Gremio,** *the* **Pedant, Lucentio, Bianca, Petruchio, Katherina, Hortensio,** *and the* **Widow** *enter.* **Tranio** *follows, with* **Biondello, Grumio,** *and other* **Servants** *bringing in the food and drink for the feast.*]

Lucentio   [*joyfully*] Finally, our disagreements are settled, although it took a long time. And it is time, when a war is over, to laugh at narrow escapes and dangers that are no more.

[*to* **Bianca**] My lovely Bianca, welcome my father while I with equal kindness welcome yours.

[*to* **Petruchio, Katherina, Hortensio,** *and* **Widow**] Brother Petruchio, sister Katherina, and you, Hortensio, with your loving Widow, thoroughly enjoy this banquet, knowing that you are welcome in my house. This last course, which completes the larger feast we had earlier to celebrate the wedding, will round off our meal and end our conflicts. Please, seat yourselves, for we now can sit together and chat as well as eat.

Petruchio   [*muttering under his breath*] All we do is sit and sit and eat and eat!

Baptista   [*offended*] Padua offers this courtesy, son Petruchio.

Petruchio   Padua offers nothing but kindness.

Hortensio   I wish that were true, for both our sakes.

Petruchio   Why, I do believe that Hortensio fears his widow.

Widow   Trust me, I'm not afraid of him.

Petruchio   You are very sensible not to be, but you missed my meaning. I mean that Hortensio is afraid of you.

Widow   He that is giddy thinks the world turns
20   round.

Petruchio   Roundly replied.

Katherina   Mistress, how mean you that?

Widow   Thus I conceive by him.

Petruchio   Conceives by me! how likes Hortensio that?

Hortensio   My widow says, thus she conceives her tale.

Petruchio   Very well mended. Kiss him for that, good
25   widow.

Katherina   "He that is giddy thinks the world turns
       round":
    I pray you tell me what you meant by that.

Widow   Your husband, being troubled with a shrew,
    Measures my husband's sorrow by his woe:
30   And now you know my meaning.

Katherina   A very mean meaning.

Widow   Right, I mean you.

Katherina   And I am mean indeed, respecting you.

Petruchio   To her, Kate!

Hortensio   To her, widow!

Petruchio   A hundred marks, my Kate does put her
35   down.

Hortensio   That's my office.

Widow   [*quoting a proverb*] He who is dizzy thinks the world is spinning.

Petruchio   A very frank answer.

Katherina   [*to* **Widow**] Madam, what do you mean by that?

Widow   I conceive that he is.

Petruchio   [*punning suggestively*] Conceive by me? What does Hortensio think of that?

Hortensio   My wife means that that's how she conceives her remark.

Petruchio   Very well corrected. Kiss him for that, good Widow.

Katherina   [*stiffly, knowing the* **Widow** *meant it as an insult*] "He who is dizzy thinks the world is spinning." Please tell me what you mean by that.

Widow   Your husband, being plagued by a shrew, thinks that my husband's situation is as unfortunate as his own. And now you know what I meant by that. [*She turns away, deliberately snubbing* **Katherina**.]

Katherina   That's a very mean meaning.

Widow   [*over her shoulder*] That's right, I do mean you.

Katherina   Yet, compared to you, I'm easygoing.

Petruchio   Have at her, Katherina!

Hortensio   [*not to be outdone*] Have at her, Widow!

Petruchio   I'll wager one hundred gold coins that my Kate can lay her out.

Hortensio   [*sniggering at his own double entendre*] That's *my* office.

Petruchio   Spoke like an officer. Ha' to thee, lad!

Drinks to Hortensio.

Baptista   How likes Gremio these quick-witted folks?

39 **Gremio**   Believe me, sir, they butt together well.

Bianca   Head, and butt! an hasty-witted body
Would say your head and butt were head and horn.

Vincentio   Ay, mistress bride, hath that awakened you?

Bianca   Ay, but not frighted me, therefore I'll sleep
again.

Petruchio   Nay, that you shall not, since you have begun;
45   Have at you for a [bitter] jest or two!

Bianca   Am I your bird? I mean to shift my bush,
And then pursue me as you draw your bow.
You are welcome all.

Exeunt Bianca [with Katherina, and Widow].

Petruchio   She hath prevented me. Here, Signior Tranio,
50   This bird you aim'd at, though you hit her not;
Therefore a health to all that shot and miss'd.

Tranio   O, sir, Lucentio slipp'd me like his greyhound,
Which runs himself, and catches for his master.

Petruchio   A good swift simile, but something currish.

Petruchio   [*Laughing uproariously and slapping* **Hortensio** *on the back,* **Petruchio** *puns on "office" and "officer."*] Spoken like an officer! Here's to you, pal! [**Petruchio** *drinks to* **Hortensio**.]

Baptista   How do you like these quick-witted folks, Gremio?

Gremio   They certainly like to butt heads, sir.

Bianca   Head and butt! A clever person would say that those who butt heads are likely to end up with horns on their heads. [*She refers to "cuckolding," in which a husband whose wife has been unfaithful was publicly humiliated by being forced to wear horns on his head.*]

Vincentio   Ah, lady-bride, has that subject awakened you?

Bianca   Yes, but not frightened me, so I'll go back to sleep.

Petruchio   Oh, no, you won't! Since you've started this, I'll respond to your pointed jokes.

Bianca   Am I the bird you're taking aim at? Then I'll fly to another bush, and you'll have to aim at me as you draw your bow.

[*to all guests*] We welcome you all here.

[**Bianca**, **Katherina**, *the* **Widow**, *and all the female guests leave the room*.]

Petruchio   She has gotten away from me. You, Signior Tranio, also took aim at that bird although you missed her.

[*loudly, to all guests present*] Here's a toast to all who aimed at her but missed!

Tranio   Oh, well, sir, Lucentio let me off my leash, like a greyhound that chases the prey to capture it for his master.

Petruchio   [*punning*] A good, quick simile, but rather dogged.

Tranio   'Tis well, sir, that you hunted for yourself;
56   'Tis thought your deer does hold you at a bay.

Baptista   O, O, Petruchio, Tranio hits you now.

Lucentio   I thank thee for that gird, good Tranio.

Hortensio   Confess, confess, hath he not hit you here?

60 **Petruchio**   'A has a little gall'd me, I confess;
And as the jest did glance away from me,
'Tis ten to one it maim'd you [two] outright.

Baptista   Now in good sadness, son Petruchio,
I think thou hast the veriest shrew of all.

Petruchio   Well, I say no; and therefore [for] assurance
66   Let's each one send unto his wife,
And he whose wife is most obedient,
To come at first when he doth send for her,
Shall win the wager which we will propose.

Hortensio   Content. What's the wager?

Lucentio   Twenty crowns.

71 **Petruchio**   Twenty crowns!
I'll venture so much of my hawk or hound,
But twenty times so much upon my wife.

Lucentio   A hundred then.

Hortensio   Content.

Petruchio   A match! 'tis done.

Hortensio   Who shall begin?

75 **Lucentio**   That will I.
Go, Biondello, bid your mistress come to me.

Tranio   It's a good thing that you hunted for yourself. Some think your deer faces you down.

Baptista   [*laughing loudly*] Ha, Petruchio! Tranio got you that time!

Lucentio   [*laughing*] Thank you, Tranio, for that hit.

Hortensio   [*laughing and wiping his eyes*] Admit it! He got you that time.

Petruchio   He has bruised me a little, I admit. [*As the others laugh even harder, he turns the tables.*] But when the joke bounced off me, ten to one it hit one of you two right between the eyes.

Baptista   [*shaking his head regretfully*] But, in all seriousness, son Petruchio, I think you really do have the worst shrew of all.

Petruchio   Well, I say that I don't. In fact, to prove it, let's each send for his wife. The one whose wife is the most obedient to come quickly when he sends for her shall win the bet which we shall agree upon.

Hortensio   Fine. How much is the bet?

Lucentio   Twenty gold coins.

Petruchio   Twenty gold coins? I would bet that much on my hawk or my hound. I would bet twenty times that on my wife.

Lucentio   One hundred, then.

Hortensio   Fine.

Petruchio   It's a bet, then.

Hortensio   Who shall go first?

Lucentio   I will.

Biondello   I go.

Exit.

Baptista   Son, I'll be your half, Bianca comes.

Lucentio   I'll have no halves; I'll bear it all myself.

Enter **Biondello**.

How now, what news?

Biondello   Sir, my mistress sends you word
81   That she is busy, and she cannot come.

Petruchio   How? she is busy and she cannot come!
Is that an answer?

Gremio   Ay, and a kind one too.
Pray God, sir, your wife send you not a worse.

85 **Petruchio**   I hope better.

Hortensio   Sirrah Biondello, go and entreat my wife
To come to me forthwith.

Exit Biondello.

Petruchio   O ho, entreat her!
Nay then she must needs come.

Hortensio   I am afraid, sir,
Do what you can, yours will not be entreated.

Enter **Biondello**.

90   Now, where's my wife?

Biondello   She says you have some goodly jest in hand.
She will not come; she bids you come to her.

[*to* **Biondello**] Go, Biondello, tell Bianca to come to me.

Biondello   I'm going.

[**Biondello** *leaves.*]

Baptista   [*to* **Lucentio**] Son, I'll split the bet with you that Bianca comes.

Lucentio   [*confidently*] I don't need to go halves. I'll cover the whole bet myself.

[**Biondello** *returns.*]

Well, what's the news?

Biondello   Sir, my mistress says to tell you that she is busy and cannot come.

Petruchio   [*laughing at* **Lucentio's** *obvious embarrassment*] What? "She is busy and cannot come?" Is that an answer?

Gremio   Yes, and a kind one, at that. Pray to God, sir, that your wife doesn't send you a worse one.

Petruchio   I hope for better.

Hortensio   [*nervously*] Biondello, go and request that my wife come to me right away.

[**Biondello** *leaves.*]

Petruchio   Oh-ho! *Request*? Then she must certainly come.

Hortensio   I'm afraid, sir, that whatever you do, yours will not come at your request.

[**Biondello** *returns.*]

[*to* **Biondello**] Now, where's my wife?

Petruchio Worse and worse; she will not come! O vild,
Intolerable, not to be endur'd!
95 Sirrah Grumio, go to your mistress,
Say I command her to come to me.

Exit [Grumio].

Hortensio I know her answer.

Petruchio   What?

Hortensio   She will not.

Petruchio The fouler fortune mine, and there an end.

Enter **Katherina**.

Baptista Now, by my holidam, here comes Katherina!

100 **Katherina** What is your will, sir, that you send for me?

Petruchio Where is your sister, and Hortensio's wife?

Katherina They sit conferring by the parlor fire.

Petruchio Go fetch them hither. If they deny to come,
Swinge me them soundly forth unto their husbands.
105 Away, I say, and bring them hither straight.

[Exit Katherina.]

Lucentio Here is a wonder, if you talk of a wonder.

Hortensio And so it is; I wonder what it bodes.

Petruchio Marry, peace it bodes, and love, and quiet life,
An aweful rule, and right supremacy;
And, to be short, what not, that's sweet and happy.

Biondello   [*trying to hide his amusement*] She says you must be joking. She will not come. She says you should go to her.

Petruchio   It gets worse and worse. She *will not* come! It's disgusting, intolerable, unbearable!

[*to* **Grumio**] Grumio, go to your mistress. Say that I *command* her to come to me.

[**Grumio** *leaves.*]

Hortensio   [*snidely, miffed at looking foolish*] I know what her answer will be.

Petruchio   What?

Hortensio   She will not come.

Petruchio   [*shrugging unconcernedly*] My worse luck, if that's so.

Baptista   [*in amazement*] Now, by the Virgin, here comes Katherina!

[**Katherina** *returns.*]

Katherina   What do you want, sir, that you sent for me?

Petruchio   Where are your sister and Hortensio's wife?

Katherina   They're sitting chatting by the parlor fire.

Petruchio   Go bring them here. If they refuse to come, chase them to their husbands here with a whip. Go, I tell you, and bring them here right away.

[**Katherina** *leaves.*]

Lucentio   This is a miracle, if you wish to speak of miracles.

Hortensio   It certainly is. I wonder what it means.

111 **Baptista**   Now fair befall thee, good Petruchio!
　　　　The wager thou hast won, and I will add
　　　　Unto their losses twenty thousand crowns,
　　　　Another dowry to another daughter,
115 　　For she is chang'd, as she had never been.

　　Petruchio   Nay, I will win my wager better yet,
　　　　And show more sign of her obedience,
　　　　Her new-built virtue and obedience.

　　Enter **Kate**, **Bianca**, *and* **Widow**.

　　　　See where she comes, and brings your froward wives
120 　　As prisoners to her womanly persuasion.
　　　　Katherine, that cap of yours becomes you not;
　　　　Off with that bable, throw it under-foot.

　　　　　　　　　　[*Katherina throws down her cap.*]

　　Widow   Lord, let me never have a cause to sigh,
　　　　Till I be brought to such a silly pass!

125 **Bianca**   Fie, what a foolish duty call you this?

　　Lucentio   I would your duty were as foolish too.
　　　　The wisdom of your duty, fair Bianca,
　　　　Hath cost me [a] hundred crowns since supper-time.

　　Bianca   The more fool you for laying on my duty.

　　Petruchio   Katherine, I charge thee tell these head-
130 　　strong women
　　　　What duty they do owe their lords and husbands.

　　Widow   Come, come, you're mocking; we will have no telling.

　　Petruchio   Come on, I say, and first begin with her.

　　Widow   She shall not.

Petruchio   Indeed, it means peace and love and a quiet life, reverence and a legitimate supremacy, and to put it briefly, all that is sweet and happy.

Baptista   Now, may good luck come to you, good Petruchio! You've won the bet, and I will add to their losses another twenty thousand gold coins, another dowry for another daughter, for she is transformed as if she had never existed.

Petruchio   No, I'll better my win and demonstrate her newly created virtue and obedience even more.

[*to* **Lucentio** *and* **Hortensio**] See, here she comes, bringing your two headstrong wives, prisoners to her feminine persuasiveness.

[**Katherina** *returns, bringing* **Bianca** *and the* **Widow**.]

[*to* **Katherina**] Katherina, that hat of yours doesn't look good on you. Take it off and throw it on the ground.

[**Katherina** *immediately throws her hat on the ground*.]

Widow   Lord, I'm as likely never to have a sad day in my life as I am to be reduced to such a state!

Bianca   [*to* **Katherina**] Shame on you! What foolish kind of obedience do you call this?

Lucentio   [*disgruntled*] I wish you were as foolishly obedient as she is. The "wisdom" of your idea of wifely duty has cost me one hundred gold coins since suppertime.

Bianca   [*tartly*] The more fool you then for betting on my obedience.

Petruchio   Katherina, I order you to tell these obstinate women what their duty to their husbands is.

Widow   Come, come, you're joking. We won't be lectured to.

135 **Petruchio**   I say she shall, and first begin with her.

Katherina   Fie, fie, unknit that threat'ning unkind brow,
And dart not scornful glances from those eyes,
To wound thy lord, thy king, thy governor.
It blots thy beauty, as frosts do bite the meads,
Confounds thy fame, as whirlwinds shake fair buds,
141 And in no sense is meet or amiable.
A woman mov'd is like a fountain troubled,
Muddy, ill-seeming, thick, bereft of beauty,
And while it is so, none so dry or thirsty
145 Will deign to sip, or touch one drop of it.
Thy husband is thy lord, thy life, thy keeper,
Thy head, thy sovereign; one that cares for thee,
And for thy maintenance; commits his body
To painful labor, both by sea and land;
150 To watch the night in storms, the day in cold,
Whilst thou li'st warm at home, secure and safe;
And craves no other tribute at thy hands
But love, fair looks, and true obedience—
Too little payment for so great a debt.
155 Such duty as the subject owes the prince,
Even such a woman oweth to her husband;
And when she is froward, peevish, sullen, sour,
And not obedient to his honest will,
What is she but a foul contending rebel,
160 And graceless traitor to her loving lord?
I am asham'd that women are so simple
To offer war where they should kneel for peace,
Or seek for rule, supremacy, and sway,
When they are bound to serve, love, and obey.
165 Why are our bodies soft, and weak, and smooth,
Unapt to toil and trouble in the world,
But that our soft conditions, and our hearts,
Should well agree with our external parts?
Come, come, you froward and unable worms!

Petruchio Go on, I tell you, and begin with her.

Widow Oh, no, she won't.

Petruchio I say she will.

[*to* **Katherina**] Begin with her.

Katherina Shame on you! Shame on you! Remove the frown from your face and don't let those scornful looks dart from your eyes. They injure your lord, your king, your monarch. Looking that way mars your beauty as frosts blight the meadows and damages your reputation as whirlwinds shake the spring buds. It is neither proper nor pleasant. An angry woman is like a stirred up stream: muddy, unappealing, sluggish, ugly. And when a stream is like that, no one, no matter how thirsty, would be willing to sip from it or even touch it. Your husband is your lord, your life, your protector, your head, your ruler. He takes care of you and devotes himself to difficult labor both on land and at sea to provide for you, enduring the storms at night and the cold of the day while you are at home, warm and safe in your bed. And he asks nothing more from you than love, pleasant looks, and true obedience, too little payment for all that he is owed. A wife owes her husband the same duty that a subject owes a prince. And when she is uncooperative, irritable, sullen, sour, and disobedient to his honest wishes, what is she but a wicked, willful rebel and a contemptible traitor to her loving lord? I am ashamed that women are so stupid that they would fight when they should go on their knees to beg for peace, or struggle to rule, to be the boss and give the orders, when they should serve, love, and obey. Why are women's bodies soft and weak and smooth, unsuited to the hard labor and troubles of the world, if not that our soft external parts should harmonize with our soft natures and our hearts? Come, come, you stubborn and weak worms! I have been as full of myself as either of you,

170 My mind hath been as big as one of yours,
My heart as great, my reason haply more,
To bandy word for word and frown for frown;
But now I see our lances are but straws,
Our strength as weak, our weakness past compare,
That seeming to be most which we indeed least are.
176 Then vail your stomachs, for it is no boot,
And place your hands below your husband's foot;
In token of which duty, if he please,
My hand is ready, may it do him ease.

Petruchio   Why, there's a wench! Come on, and kiss
180 me, Kate.

Lucentio   Well, go thy ways, old lad, for thou shalt ha't.

Vincentio   'Tis a good hearing when children are toward.

Lucentio   But a harsh hearing when women are froward.

Petruchio   Come, Kate, we'll to bed.
185 We three are married, but you two are sped.

[*To Lucentio.*]

'Twas I won the wager, though you hit the white,
And being a winner, God give you good night!

Exeunt Petruchio [with Katherina].

Hortensio   Now go thy ways, thou hast tam'd a curst shrow.

Lucentio   'Tis a wonder, by your leave, she will be tam'd so.

[*Exeunt.*]

my heart as arrogant, my thinking perhaps even more so, slinging words and frowns back and forth. But now I see that our weapons are as weak as pieces of straw, our strength just that weak, our weakness indescribable, so that what we seem to be is the last thing that we are. So lower your pride, for it is useless, and place your hands beneath your husband's foot. And, as a sign of my wifely duty, my hand is ready to bring him comfort, if he wishes it.

Petruchio   Why, there's a good woman! Come on and kiss me, Kate.

Lucentio   [*with grudging admiration*] Well, carry on, old fellow, for you have won the bet.

Vincentio   It's good to hear of it when children are well behaved.

Lucentio   [*glumly*] But not good to hear of it when women are obstinate.

Petruchio   Come, Kate, let's go to bed.

[*to* **Lucentio** *and* **Hortensio**] The three of us are married, but you two are done for.

[*to* **Lucentio**] I won the bet even though your arrow hit the white of the target, and so being a winner, I bid you goodnight! [**"Bianca"** *means "white"*]

[**Petruchio** *and* **Katherina** *leave.*]

Hortensio   [*to the now-absent* **Petruchio**] Well, run along. You have tamed a terrible shrew.

Lucentio   [*shaking his head in mystification*] It's hard to believe, if you don't mind my saying so, that she let herself be tamed so thoroughly.

[*All leave.*]

Activities

Structure

The Induction

Discuss the Induction of *The Taming of the Shrew*. These are some questions you will find helpful in doing so.

1   Some experts believe that Shakespeare intended Katherina to be a parallel character to Christopher Sly, whereas others think that Petruchio is the intended parallel. Which view do you agree with? Why do you think so?

2   What parallels can you observe between Petruchio and the Lord in the Induction? What similarities can you see in other characters in the Induction and those in the main action of the play? What implications do these parallels have on the themes of the play?

3   Why does Shakespeare *not* include a scene at the end of the play with Christopher Sly and the other characters from the Induction? How does this decision affect the theme of female submission?

4   Does the Induction support or undermine the idea that women should be submissive to men? Why do you think so?

Comic Elements

Shakespeare includes many standard comic elements in *The Taming of the Shrew*, such as stock characters, disguise and/or mistaken identity, and discrepancy of awareness.

Stock characters

Stock characters are characters who tend to behave in stereo-typical ways; writers usually use the audience's expectations for how the character will act to create humorous dialog or actions.

Here are some examples of stock characters:

- the block-headed servant
- the henpecked husband
- the shrewish woman
- Pantalone (a character in Italian Renaissance *Commedia dell'Arte* who is a wealthy but foolish old man, typically married to a younger woman)
- the braggart soldier
- the innocent young girl

Which characters in *The Taming of the Shrew* can be identified as the stock characters listed above? What other stock characters can you think of? Which characters in the play represent them? Which characters behave consistently with the audience's expectations for them and which ones do not do so? Why do you suppose Shakespeare chose to have some characters behave in ways that are not typical of stock characters?

Disguise/Mistaken Identity

Another comic element that we can observe in *The Taming of the Shrew* is that of various characters' wearing disguises.

1. Which characters wear disguises during the course of the play? Why do they do so? Can you see any similarities in the situations or motivations of the characters?

2. Which characters present a false appearance even though they never wear any type of physical disguise? What do they hope to accomplish by doing so?

3. Which characters are put in dangerous situations as a result of the masquerades?

4. Do the situations that arise in these cases seem truly dangerous or simply comical? Why or why not?

Discrepancy of Awareness

Many times authors create situations in which the audience and/or some characters in the play may know things that others do not, leading to comic misunderstandings. For example, the audience knows that Lucentio and Tranio have exchanged identities so that Lucentio can try to woo Bianca; others, however, don't know this. Consequently, in Act 5, Scene 1, when Vincentio arrives and learns that Tranio is masquerading as his son, Lucentio, and the Pedant is claiming to be Vincentio, Vincentio's accusations and fears are amusing rather than alarming to the audience.

Find other examples from the play of discrepancies of awareness. Discuss which characters know something that someone else doesn't know. Also discuss whether Shakespeare uses that situation to create comedy or, conversely, to create dramatic tension.

Roman New Comedy

The Taming of the Shrew includes a plot which is structurally similar to a very old type of comedy known as "Roman New Comedy." The plot of the Roman New Comedy concerns the desire of a young couple to form a union; however, a blocking force—represented by the *senex iratus* (i.e., the angry old man) and/or the *senex matrona* (i.e., the old woman)—is keeping them from accomplishing their goal. The society in which they live, typically represented by some combination of one or both sets of their parents, is depicted as being seriously flawed or corrupt, whereas the society that the young couple hopes to establish will be significantly better than that of their elders.

- Which pair of lovers represents the typical New Comedy couple and who is/are the blocking force(s)? What other blocking forces can you identify?

- How does Shakespeare let the audience know that the society in *The Taming of the Shrew* is flawed or corrupt?
- What similarities and differences can you observe between the situations of the typical New Comedy and *The Taming of the Shrew*? Why do you suppose that Shakespeare changed certain aspects of the typical New Comedy when he used it in *The Taming of the Shrew*? How do these changes affect the theme(s) of the play?

Themes

By taking note of repeated ideas or similar situations, we can discover themes which will enhance our understanding of *The Taming of the Shrew*.

If the quotation given below is part of a longer speech, read the entire passage in which it appears in order to fully understand what is being said.

Deception

There are many instances of deception in *The Taming of the Shrew*. Read and think about these quotes and about which character is speaking the lines.

1 "Sirs, I will practice [*that is, play a trick*] on this drunken man.
   What think you, if he were convey'd to bed,
   Wrapped in sweet clothes, rings put on his fingers,
   A most delicious banquet by his bed,
   And brave attendants near him when he wakes,
   Would not the beggar then forget himself?" (Induction, Scene 1, Lines 36–41)

2 "Thou shalt be master, Tranio, in my stead;
   Keep house and port and servants as I should.
   I will some other be, some Florentine,
   Some Neapolitan, or meaner man of Pisa." (Act 1, Scene 1, Lines 202–205)

3 "I'll attend her here,
   And woo her with some spirit when she comes.
   Say that she rail, why then I'll tell her plain
   She sings as sweetly as a nightingale;
   Say that she frown, I'll say she looks as clear
   As morning roses newly wash'd with dew" (Act 2, Scene 1, lines 168–173)

- Find other examples of deception in the play. Who deceives whom, and for what reason(s)? Can you see any patterns in terms of the reasons for the deception?
- Which deceptions are done for the purpose of benefiting the deceiver?
- Which deceptions are done for selfless reasons?

Power

There are many kinds of power in evidence in *The Taming of the Shrew*. Read and think about these quotes. Which character is speaking the lines and to whom is the speaker referring?

1   "Sir, understand you this of me in sooth:
    The youngest daughter whom you hearken for,
    Her father keeps from all access of suitors,
    And will not promise her to any man,
    Until the elder sister first be wed:
    The younger then is free, and not before." (Act 1, Scene 2, lines 257–262)

2   "Her silence flouts me, and I'll be revenged." (Act 2, Scene 1, line 29)

3   "She is my goods, my chattels, she is my house,
    My household stuff, my field, my barn,
    My horse, my ox, my ass, my any thing;
    And here she stands, touch her whoever dare,
    I'll bring mine action on the proudest he
    That stops my way in Padua." (Act 3, Scene 2, lines 230–235)

- Find other examples of power in the play. What kinds of power are evident? Are any of the types of power beneficial or are they all negative? Why do you think so?
- What characters subvert or undermine the power of others?
- What differences in power can you observe at the end of the play as opposed to the beginning?
- What do you think Shakespeare was trying to say about power?

Love

There are many references to love in *The Taming of the Shrew*. Read and think about these quotes and about which character is speaking the lines.

1 "Now, by the world, it is a lusty wench!
   I love her ten times more than e'er I did.
   O, how I long to have some chat with her!" (Act 2, Scene 1, lines 160–162)

2 "For me, that I may surely keep mine oath,
   I will be married to a wealthy widow,
   Ere three days pass, which hath as long lov'd me
   As I have lov'd this proud disdainful haggard." (Act 4, Scene 2, lines 36–39)

3 "But I, who never knew how to entreat,
   Nor never needed that I should entreat,
   Am starv'd for meat, giddy for lack of sleep,
   With oaths kept waking and with brawling fed;
   And that which spites me more than all these wants,
   He does it under name of perfect love." (Act 4, Scene 3, lines 7–12)

- Find as many other references to love as you can in the play.
- Which characters say they love another character? What kinds of love are depicted in the play?
- Does anything occur that makes you doubt whether a character really loves the one he or she claims to love? Why do you suppose that Shakespeare included these situations?

Conformity versus Nonconformity

Although the word "conformity" never appears in the play, conformity to social rules is a significant aspect of *The Taming of the Shrew*. Read each of the quotes below and think about who is speaking and who is failing to conform to some social rule or expectation.

1 "Thou must be married to no man but me;
For I am he am born to tame you Kate,
And bring you from a wild Kate to a Kate
Conformable as other household Kates." (Act 2, Scene 1, lines 275–278)

2 "Why, sir, you know this is your wedding-day.
First were we sad, fearing you would not come,
Now sadder, that you come so unprovided.
Fie, doff this habit, shame to your estate,
An eye-sore to our solemn festival!" (Act 3, Scene 2, lines 97–101)

3 "I'll have no bigger: this doth fit the time,
And gentlewomen wear such caps as these." (Act 4, Scene 3, lines 69–70)

- Find other situations of or references to conformity to social rules in the play.
- What types of conformity do these quotations refer to? In other words, do the types of conformity pertain to appearance, behavior, or something else?
- Based on what you observe about conformity in the play, compare and contrast the social rules and expectations in terms of whom they apply to. How do they vary when it comes to gender and status? What social values and expectations do these variations imply?
- Do you think Shakespeare was trying to support the idea of conformity being important or not? Explain your reasons for your answer.

Shame or Shaming

Shame, a subject which is closely related to that of conformity, is either experienced by various characters in the play or inflicted on others by characters in the play. Think about these quotes and what is happening in the play when they are being spoken.

1 "Why, how now, dame! whence grows this insolence?
   Bianca, stand aside. Poor girl! she weeps.
   Go ply thy needle, meddle not with her.
   For shame, thou helding of a devilish spirit,
   Why dost thou wrong her that did ne'er wrong thee?
   When did she cross thee with a bitter word?" (Act 2, Scene 1, lines 23–28)

2 "No shame but mine: I must, forsooth, be forc'd
   To give my hand oppos'd against my heart
   Unto a mad-brain rudesby full of spleen,
   Who woo'd in haste, and means to wed at leisure." (Act 3, Scene 2, lines 8–11)

3 "And I seeing this came thence for very shame,
   And after me, I know, the rout is coming.
   Such a mad marriage never was before." (Act 3, Scene 2, lines 180–182)

- Which character is speaking each of these quotations and under what circumstances?
- What other references to shame or shaming can you find in the play (bear in mind that that word "fie" could mean "shame on you")?
- What cultural values are being reinforced or undermined in the various situations?
- What point might Shakespeare have been trying to make about shame?

Pride versus Humility

Pride and humility are mentioned frequently in the play. Read the quotations below and think about the situations involved and the characters who are speaking.

1 "Such duty to the drunkard let him do,
   With soft low tongue and lowly courtesy,
   And say, 'What is't your honour will command,
   Wherein your lady and your humble wife,
   May show her duty and make known her love?'" (Induction, Scene 1, lines 113–117)

2 "O yes, I saw sweet beauty in her face,
   Such as the daughter of Agenor had,
   That made great Jove to humble him to her hand.
   When with his knees he kiss'd the Cretan strand." (Act 1, Scene 1, lines 167–170)

3 "Well, come, my Kate; we will unto your father's
   Even in these honest mean habiliments;
   Our purses shall be proud, our garments poor,
   For 'tis the mind that makes the body rich;
   And as the sun breaks through the darkest clouds,
   So honor peereth in the meanest habit." (Act 4, Scene 3, lines 169–174)

- Find other quotations referring to pride and humility in the play.
- Who is being referred to when the word "humble" is used? What are the reasons for the person being "humble"?
- What do the various characters take pride in? How do they demonstrate their pride?
- Can you detect any differences in whether pride is considered to be positive or negative? Is pride acceptable for some persons or groups but not for others?
- What conclusions can you draw about what Shakespeare is implying about humility and pride?

Wealth and Possessions

There are numerous references to wealth and possessions throughout *The Taming of the Shrew*. Read the following passages, noting who is speaking and what circumstances they are discussing.

1   "Think'st thou, Hortensio,
   though her father be very rich, any man is so very
   a fool to be married to hell?" (Act 1, Scene 1, lines 123–125)

2   "You knew my father well, and in him me,
   Left soly heir to all his lands and goods,
   Which I have better'd rather than decreas'd:
   Then tell me, if I get your daughter's love,
   What dowry shall I have with her to wife?" (Act 2, Scene 1, lines 116–120)

3   "Content you, gentlemen: I will compound this strife:
   'Tis deeds must win the prize; and he of both
   That can assure my daughter greatest dower
   Shall have my Bianca's love." (Act 2, Scene 1, lines 341–344)

- What other quotations can you find concerning wealth or possessions in the play?
- Are there any characters to whom wealth or possessions seem unimportant? What makes you think so?
- What do the characters in *The Taming of the Shrew* view as giving women value in the play? Are attitudes about women different today, and if so how and why?
- Compare and contrast attitudes today about wealth and possessions to those of the characters in the play. To what extent are they similar or different? Do you consider the attitudes of those around you to be better than those demonstrated in the play? Why do you think so?

Obedience

Many of the characters are expected to obey others in the play. Think about who is speaking and which character is expected to obey another.

1 "In brief, sir, sith it your pleasure is,
And I am tied to be obedient—
For so your father charged me at our parting;
'Be serviceable to my son,' quoth he,
Although I think 'twas in another sense—
I am content to be Lucentio,
Because so well I love Lucentio." (Act 1, Scene 1, lines 211–217)

2 "Good Hortensio,
I bade the rascal knock upon your gate,
And could not get him for my heart to do it." (Act 1, Scene 2, lines 36–38)

3 "Another way I have to man my haggard,
To make her come and know her keeper's call,
That is, to watch her, as we watch these kites
That bate and beat and will not be obedient." (Act 4, Scene 1, lines 193–196)

- What other quotations can you find concerning obedience in the play?
- Which characters are required, according to the social standards of the time, to be obedient to other characters? What are the consequences for failure to obey? Can you observe any patterns that reveal the "pecking order" of the society in which the play is set?
- Do the characters that obey others always do so out of necessity or are there other motivations for obedience?
- What do you think Shakespeare may have been trying to say about the issue of obedience?

Teaching and Learning

The Taming of the Shrew includes many references to teaching and learning. Read and think about these quotations and the situations to which they refer.

1 "Here let us breathe and haply institute
A course of learning and ingenious studies." (Act 1, Scene 1, lines 8–9)

2 "And for I know she taketh most delight
In music, instruments, and poetry,
Schoolmasters will I keep within my house,
Fit to instruct her youth." (Act 1, Scene 1, lines 92–95)

3 "And there I stood amazed for a while,
As on a pillory, looking through the lute,
While she did call me rascal fiddler
And twangling Jack; with twenty such vild terms,
As had she studied to misuse me so." (Act 2, Scene 1, lines 155–159)

- Find other references to teaching, learning, or studying in the play. What are the various subjects and kinds of learning?
- Can you detect any patterns in the subjects which the various characters study? What cultural values do these subjects imply?
- Can you find any examples of teaching or learning that would not be among the topics taught in a formal learning situation? Do these "subjects" appear to be of more or less importance to the characters in the play than those formally taught? How can you tell?

Appetite and Eating

Eating is an activity that occurs throughout the play, and appetite is referred to both literally and figuratively. Think about the quotations below and the aspect or type of appetite or eating being referred to.

1   "Balk logic with acquaintance that you have,
    And practise rhetoric in your common talk;
    Music and poesy use to quicken you,
    The mathematics and the metaphysics,
    Fall to them as you find your stomach serves you:
    No profit grows where is no pleasure ta'en:
    In brief, sir, study what you most affect." (Act 1, Scene 1, lines 34–40)

2   "Sir, I shall not be slack: in sign whereof,
    Please ye we may contrive this afternoon,
    And quaff carouses to our mistress' health,
    And do as adversaries do in law,
    Strive mightily, but eat and drink as friends." (Act 1, Scene 2, lines 273–277)

3   "Come, Kate, sit down, I know you have a stomach." (Act 4, Scene 1, line 158)

   • There are many references to appetite and the act of eating in the play. Find other references and then determine which are meant literally and which are figurative (be sure to look at the original language when making this determination). In #3 above, for example, the word "stomach" could not only mean appetite but it could also mean stubbornness or anger.

   • Under what circumstances is eating an activity that is engaged in as a means of bringing people together? Are there any times when it is an activity that creates division between people?

   • What do you think Shakespeare's reasons were for emphasizing appetite and eating in *The Taming of the Shrew*?

Characters

Search the text to find answers to the following questions. They will help you to form opinions about the principal characters in the play. Record any relevant quotations in Shakespeare's own words.

Katherina

1   A shrew, according to lexicographer Samuel Johnson, is a "peevish, malignant, clamorous, spiteful, vexatious, turbulent woman."

   a To what extent does this description fit Katherina at the beginning of the play?

   b The other characters view Katherina very negatively at the beginning of the play. What societal values concerning women do their opinions reflect?

   c Does Shakespeare include anything when we first meet Katherina to create sympathy for her? If so, how does he do so?

2   During the course of the play, Katherina is often compared to animals.

   a Identify the different animals to which she is compared.

   b Which characters refer to her in this way?

   c What common elements can you find in terms of the types of animals to which she is compared?

   d Do you see any differences in the way Katherina is described or referred to at the beginning of the play as opposed to the end? What point do you think Shakespeare may have been trying to make by these descriptions?

3 The other characters talk about Katherina on many occasions during the play.

   a What nouns or adjectives are used to describe her? Identify who is speaking and see if you can find any patterns in the way she is described.

   b What does she say about herself? How does that compare or contrast with what others say about her?

   c Does the way she is described by others change during the course of the play, and if so why do you think the other characters change their view of her?

4 In his essay "Bewitching the Shrew," Robert M. Schuler observes that in Shakespeare's time shrewish women were closely associated with witches in the public mind.

   a People once believed that one indication that a woman was a witch was the fact that everything she said or did was "contrary" (that is, the opposite of what she was supposed to do). Find examples of Katherina's saying and doing things that could be considered "contrary."

   b Find examples of Katherina's being called names such as "fiend of hell" and other words associated with hell and the devil.

   c In some medieval mystery plays (that is, plays which depict events from the Bible such as the Fall of Man or Noah and the Flood), the devil would actually marry a shrew. Relate this circumstance to the characters and theme(s) of the play.

   d In Katherina's lecture on a wife's duty to her husband, she denounces any woman who is a "foul contending rebel." How might this reference to a rebel be linked to the devil?

5 At times, Katherina threatens others and/or behaves violently.

   a What violent actions does she actually perform? Against whom does she enact violence? For what reason(s)?

   b Whom does she threaten with violence without acting upon her threat? Why do you suppose that she merely threatens violence at times?

   c Does her attitude toward violence change during the course of the play? What makes you think so?

6 Even though Katherina is viewed negatively by those around her, she also has positive qualities.

   a List as many positive qualities for Katherina as you can think of.

   b Find examples from the play for each positive quality.

   c How do these qualities affect your view of her?

7 Although Katherina declares that she will not marry Petruchio, she ends up doing so anyway.

   a Are there any indications that she really does want to marry him? If so, what are they?

   b Why might she be willing to marry a man who is essentially a stranger to her?

   c Is there any indication that she is aware of the financial bargain between her father and Petruchio?

   d How and why do her interactions with Petruchio affect her overall attitudes and her behavior toward others?

Bianca

1 Bianca is the younger daughter of Baptista, sister to Katherina. Initially, the other characters view Bianca favorably, whereas Katherina is held in contempt.

   a Compare and contrast Bianca and Katherina. In what ways are they similar? How are they different?

    b How do the other characters in the play view the two sisters? What attitudes toward women and their behavior do the views of the other characters reflect?

    c Do you view Bianca in the same way that the other characters see her at the beginning of the play? Explain your reasons.

    d Does Shakespeare include any speeches or actions at the beginning of the play to undermine the audience's favorable impression of Bianca? If so, what are these things?

2   At the end of the play, Bianca appears to have changed from the character that she appeared to be at the beginning of the play.

    a In what way(s) is Bianca different?

    b In your opinion, do these changes seem to indicate that she and Lucentio will have a happy marriage? Do you think that the characters in the play would agree with you? Why or why not? Do you think that Shakespeare himself would agree with you?

3   In an earlier play that was likely Shakespeare's source for the Bianca/Lucentio plot, the character who was the parallel character of Bianca was named Polynesta. This character is different from Bianca in that she is depicted as being promiscuous, with the result that she is pregnant. Also, Polynesta has a much smaller role in the play than Bianca has.

    a Why do you suppose Shakespeare made these changes? How would the play have been different and what other changes would Shakespeare have had to make to accommodate these differences?

    b Do you think that the way Bianca is depicted makes the play stronger or weaker? What are your reasons for thinking so?

Petruchio

1 Petruchio is a character with many obvious flaws, yet he is well liked by his peers.

   a Make a list of the character traits you see in Petruchio. How many negative traits does he have? How many positive traits does he have?

   b How do the other men in the story view Petruchio? Make a list of the nouns and adjectives that the other men in the story use to describe him. Can you see any patterns in the way he is viewed, either by his peers or by those who are subordinate to him?

   c How does Petruchio's behavior differ from Katherina's? What similarities do you see in the way they act? What social expectations for female behavior as opposed to male behavior do the reactions of others indicate?

2 Upon learning about Katherina from Hortensio, Petruchio declares that the only thing he is looking for in a wife is wealth.

   a Petruchio then tells Hortensio that he will marry her even if Katherina is as ugly as the legendary woman loved by Florentius. According to the story, when Florentius agrees to be ruled by her, the ugly hag is transformed into a beautiful woman. Why do you think Shakespeare decided to have Petruchio make this comparison?

   b How does this story reflect upon the issue of female submission?

3 Money is extremely important to Petruchio.

   a What types of activities does he undertake to get more money? Are any of them immoral, illegal, or socially unacceptable for the time in which the play is set?

   b Do modern audiences view any of these activities differently from the way playgoers of Shakespeare's time probably did? Why or why not?

4 Petruchio is clearly accustomed to using force to get what he wants.

   a Find examples of Petruchio's use of force in the play.

   b Find examples in which Petruchio uses means other than physical force to get what he wants. What other methods does he use? Does the fact that he doesn't use force in these situations make his character any more or less likeable than if he had used force in those situations?

5 In a soliloquy (that is, a speech spoken by a character who is alone on stage that reveals his or her thoughts or intentions to the audience), Petruchio says that he intends to woo Katherina by acting as though everything she says and does is delightful, even when it isn't. (Act 2, Scene 1, lines 168–180)

   a Why do you think Shakespeare has Petruchio explain his actions in this soliloquy?

   b Find other soliloquies spoken by Petruchio. What does the audience learn about him in these soliloquies that they might otherwise not realize?

   c Are there any scenes in the play in which you think Petruchio is *not* putting on an act but is actually behaving in a genuine manner? Does his personality or behavior differ in those scenes from the way he usually acts, and if so how?

6 Some scholars believe that Petruchio behaves as he does in order to show Katherina how excessive and unacceptable her own behavior is.

   a Do you agree or disagree with this idea? Why or why not?

   b Does Katherina's behavior change after seeing Petruchio's outrageous behavior? To what extent do you think her behavior is actually influenced by his? Explain your reasons for thinking as you do about this issue.

7 In "Bewitching the Shrew," Robert M. Schuler notes similarities between Petruchio's character and Vice, a stock character which appeared in many medieval morality plays (that is, allegorical plays performed in order to teach moral lessons).

   a The character of Vice was noted for operating by a "contrariety principle" (Schuler), in that he said or did the opposite of that which was true or right. Vice also was noted for being a tempter of other characters in the plays. Find examples of Petruchio's behavior that would qualify as acting in these ways.

   b During his description of the wedding of Katherina and Petruchio, Gremio calls Petruchio "a devil, a devil, a very fiend" (Act 3, Scene 2, line 155). Find other evidence in the play, either in the things Petruchio is called or the way he behaves, that links him to a demonic character such as Vice. What do you think Shakespeare's intention was in having Petruchio behave as he does? Does this depiction support or undermine the concept of male dominance in the play?

   c Vice was often associated with specific sins, such as lust or drunkenness. Based upon what Petruchio says and does, what "sins" might be associated with him? Do these attributes cause the other characters to look down on Petruchio? Explain why you think so.

Lucentio

1 Lucentio is the handsome young man who comes to Padua intending to study, but instead he falls in love with Bianca.

   a Compare and contrast him with Hortensio and Gremio in terms of age, social standing, wealth, and any other aspects of his personality or life that you can think of.

   b What reasons do you think Shakespeare may have had for including other rivals for Bianca's love?

2 Lucentio and Tranio exchange identities early in the play.

   a Does anyone ever question whether they are who they claim to be? Support your answer with examples and quotations from the play.

   b How does this situation reflect on the hierarchical nature of British society at the time that Shakespeare wrote *The Taming of the Shrew*?

3 Although both Lucentio and Petruchio are wealthy noblemen, they are very different characters.

   a Compare and contrast Lucentio and Petruchio.

   b How would the play have been different if Lucentio had been matched up with Katherina, and Petruchio with Bianca? How would such a pairing change the ending of the play?

Baptista

1 Baptista, the father of Katherina and Bianca, is a wealthy citizen of Padua. He refuses to allow Bianca to wed before Katherina even though many suitors are competing for Bianca's hand.

   a What are the ways in which Baptista appears to show preference for Bianca? Does he ever favor Katherina over Bianca, and, if so, under what circumstances?

   b What are the ways in which Baptista demonstrates his love for his daughters? Based on these things, what conclusions can you draw concerning his character? What cultural values do his actions imply?

2 Most of the time, Baptista appears to be a shrewd businessman, yet there are times when his decisions seem to be less wise.

   a List the occasions on which Baptista shows sound judgment in terms of finances. List the occasions when he seems to be using poor judgment. What reasons do you think Shakespeare had for this apparent contradiction in Baptista's character?

   b When Petruchio tells Baptista that he wants to marry Katherina, Baptista says that they may marry, "[W]hen the special thing is well obtain'd, / That is, her love; for that is all in all" (Act 2, Scene 1, lines 128–129). When he is discussing Bianca's future marriage with Tranio (who is masquerading as Lucentio) and Gremio, he says:

> Content you, gentlemen, I will compound this strife.
> 'Tis deeds must win the prize, and he of both
> That can assure my daughter greatest dower
> Shall have my Bianca's love. (Act 2, Scene 1, lines 341–344)

In what ways do these two statements differ in terms of Baptista's expectations and attitudes towards his daughters? Are his expectations fulfilled by the events of the play or not? What do you think this situation shows about his relationships with Katherina and Bianca?

3 Based on the way Katherina and Bianca behave at the end of the play, do you think that Baptista's relationships with his daughters will be different in the future? Why do you think so? How will their relationships be different?

Examination/Discussion Questions

The following questions may be used either for examinations or for class discussion.

1   In the Induction, Christopher Sly suddenly stops protesting that he is not a nobleman. Why do you think he changes his mind? What changes do you observe in the way he speaks or acts after deciding that he must indeed be a nobleman?

2   A number of paintings are described to Sly in the Induction. What do these paintings have in common? What do you think the other characters hoped to accomplish by going to such lengths to describe them to him?

3   The Induction is almost never included when *The Taming of the Shrew* is performed. Why do you think that directors usually omit the Induction? Does doing so affect the themes, such as that of female submission, in the play, and, if so, how?

4   As Baptista, Katherina, Bianca, and Bianca's suitors come bustling on the scene, Tranio speculates to Lucentio that they are "some show to welcome us to town" (Act 1, Scene 1, line 47). He and Lucentio then stand aside to watch the "show." As a result, the audience is in essence watching a play within a play within a play. Find other examples in *The Taming of the Shrew* in which people watch others as they put on a "show" of some sort. Why do you suppose that Shakespeare includes this element in the play? Does this element affect the theme(s) of the play, and, if so, how?

5   Discuss Baptista Minola as a father. Do you think he is a good, loving father? Is his treatment of both his daughters equal or not? Support your answers with examples and quotations from the play.

6 Based on the action of the play, determine what the social conventions or rules of courtship and dating were in Shakespeare's time. Compare and contrast those "rules" of behavior to those of today. Can you see any advantages to those of Shakespeare's time? Why or why not?

7 When Grumio refuses to "knock" Petruchio, and Petruchio beats him for his disobedience, Grumio protests to Hortensio that the way Petruchio has mistreated him gives him legal grounds for leaving Petruchio. Bearing in mind Katherina's statement about wives being obedient to their husbands' "honest will" (Act 5, Scene 2, line 158) in her speech about the duty of a wife to her husband, do you think Shakespeare intended the audience to observe any parallels between the situations? If so, what conclusions do you think he intended the audience to draw?

8 According to Grumio, the worst thing that a woman could be called at that time was a shrew. In contrast, the worst thing a man could be called was a cuckold (that is, a man whose wife has been sexually unfaithful). In either situation, the person underwent an informal ceremony of public humiliation. What cultural values and expectations do these actions reflect? Have cultural values changed, and if so how and to what extent?

9 In Act 2, Scene 1, line 258, Petruchio compares Katherina to the Roman goddess Diana. What might his reference to Diana tell us either about how he sees Katherina or how we as the members of the audience are supposed to see her? Find other references in the play in which characters are compared to mythological beings and explain what those comparisons tell us about the one being so described, as well as what the comparison tells us about the person making the statement.

10   When Katherina and Petruchio first meet, Katherina argues
     or responds to everything that Petruchio says. However,
     when Petruchio tells Baptista, Gremio, and Tranio (who is
     impersonating Lucentio) that he and Katherina will marry
     the following Sunday, after she says that she will "see [him]
     hanged on Sunday first," Katherina abruptly stops speak-
     ing, apparently silenced by Petruchio. Find other scenes in
     the play in which Katherina appears to be silenced by Petru-
     chio. What do you infer about Elizabethan attitudes about
     women's expressing their opinions?

11   There are some experts who believe that Petruchio and
     Katherina fall in love at first sight. What do you think they
     are basing their opinion on? Do you agree or disagree with
     them? What are your reasons for thinking so?

12   At first glance, when Baptista tells Gremio and Tranio that
     "deeds must win the prize" (Act 2, Scene 1, line 342), he
     seems to be saying that what they do will determine who
     will win Bianca, but "deeds" could also refer to legal doc-
     uments or contracts. What other meaning(s) might this
     interpretation give to what Baptista is saying?

13   When Petruchio arrives for the wedding, not only is he very
     late but he is also dressed in what amounts to rags. Why do
     you think he does this? How do these things fit in with his
     plan to "tame" Katherina?

14   The way Petruchio is dressed and the way his horse looks
     when he arrives for the wedding are described in great
     detail by Biondello. Find examples in the play in which
     Shakespeare has certain events described by someone
     rather than being acted out. Why do you think he has the
     characters describe these scenes rather than have those
     involved in the event act them out? If you were the direc-
     tor of a movie version of *The Taming of the Shrew*, how would
     you handle these scenes? In other words, would you show
     the actions or have a character describe the scenes or would
     you do both? Explain your reasons for your decisions.

15 When Gremio says of Katherina, "Tut, she's a lamb, a dove, a fool to him!" (Act 3, Scene 2, Line 157), how does this compare to the way he has described her in the past? What has happened to change his opinion of her? How does this situation fit in with the theme of female submission?

16 Some scholars think that when Katherina "entreats" Petruchio not to leave before the wedding feast, Petruchio is taken by surprise that she has done so (Act 3, Scene 2, line 200). Do you agree or disagree with them? Explain your reasons for thinking so.

17 In falconry, in order to make the bird obey him, the trainer would deprive it of sleep. Also, he (trainers were virtually always men) would cover its head with a hood to control its waking and sleeping as well as to increase its dependency on him. Furthermore, the trainer would withhold food to increase the falcon's willingness to hunt. Falcon training manuals of the time also encouraged the trainer to establish a "loving" relationship with the falcon (Benson). In Act 4, Scene 1, lines 190–196, Petruchio refers to Katherina as his "falcon." Shakespeare scholar Helga Ramsey-Kurz notes that there are similarities between Petruchio's methods for taming Katherina and those used by trainers of falcons. What are these similarities in Petruchio's relationship with Katherina and that of the trainer and the falcon? What do you think Shakespeare's reasons for emphasizing these similarities were?

18 According to Margaret Ranald, the relationship of the falcon and the trainer is mutually beneficial (119–120). Do you think that Shakespeare intended to convey the idea that a marital relationship like that of Petruchio and Katherina was beneficial to both parties involved? Why or why not?

19 A haggard was a wild hawk that had been captured for the purpose of training it to hunt; these birds were superior hunters to those born in captivity, but they were far more difficult to train and more likely to fly away, never to return. At one point, Hortensio refers to Bianca as a "proud disdainful haggard" (Act 4, Scene 2, line 39). Find other references to the women in the play that are derived from the sport of hawking and discuss how and to what extent these other statements reflect on the theme of female submission.

20 A shrew is actually a small, mouse-like animal with a long snout. Sean Benson points out, "[T]he small land shrew [is] a favorite prey of hawks." However, he also notes: "[S]hrews are not tamed, but killed" (n. 37). Does the fact that Katherina is compared to both a shrew and a falcon reflect on the issue of the "taming" of women? How does it do so?

21 Tranio, disguised as Lucentio, has a discussion with Hortensio in Act 4, Scene 2 concerning whether or not Bianca cares for him, saying, "I tell you, sir, she bears me fair in hand" (line 3). Although that line can be interpreted as meaning that Tranio believes that Bianca favors him over her other suitors, it could also mean that he believes that Bianca is deceiving him or leading him on. Which interpretation of the line do you think is more accurate? Or do you think that Shakespeare intended it to be ambiguous? Why do you think so?

22 Because Bianca has shown that she is in love with "Cambio" (Lucentio, in disguise), Hortensio tells Tranio that he has decided to marry the "lusty widow." What are his reasons for marrying her? How do these reasons appear to affect the balance of power in their future relationship? Do the widow's actions in the final scene of the play indicate that the balance of power between them will be what you would expect it to be or not?

23 When Tranio tells Bianca that Hortensio intends to tame the widow he has decided to marry, she replies, "He says so, Tranio" (Act 4, Scene 2, line 53). This comment of Bianca's is an example of foreshadowing (that is, something in a literary work that indicates a future event or action). What does this incident foreshadow in the play? Find other examples of foreshadowing in *The Taming of the Shrew*. Why do you think Shakespeare included these events or speeches?

24 When Katherina and Petruchio are returning to Padua for Bianca's wedding, Petruchio tests Katherina's obedience by claiming that the sun is the moon, and then, when she agrees with him, changing his mind and saying that the sun is indeed the sun. Katherina replies, "Then, God be blest, it is the blessed sun, / But sun it is not, when you say it is not; / And the moon changes even as your mind" (Act 4, Scene 5, lines 19–21). Since, according to *The Riverside Shakespeare*, at that time the moon was believed to affect the moods of lunatics, what purpose might these lines serve in the play other than that of showing Katherina's apparent agreement with Petruchio?

25 Although in the scene discussed in Question 24 Katherina agrees with Petruchio that the sun is the moon, the fact is that the sun was the sun no matter what Petruchio insisted. That being the case, what does this aspect of the scene imply about female submission? Why do you think so?

26 Near the end of the play, Lucentio makes arrangements, with the help of his servant Biondello, to secretly marry Bianca. However, after Biondello leaves the scene, Lucentio, talking to himself, says:

> I may, and will [come to the church], if [Bianca] be so contented.
> She will be pleas'd; then wherefore should I doubt?
> Hap what hap may, I'll roundly go about her,
> It shall go hard if Cambio go without her. (Act 4, Scene 4, lines 105–108)

What do you think is the source of his sudden doubt that Bianca will marry him? How does Lucentio's doubt fit in with the issue of power in the play?

27 There are a number of examples of irony in *The Taming of the Shrew*. For example, based upon Bianca's and the Widow's refusal to obey their husbands, it seems as if, ironically, Lucentio and Hortensio have unwittingly married shrews in that, in contrast to Katherina's obedience, their "disobedience" cast them in the role of shrew. What other examples of irony can you find in the play? Do these examples reflect on any of the themes of the play, and if so how?

28 In literature, characters can be either static or dynamic. Static characters are those who fail to change or grow during the course of a story, play, or poem; oftentimes their failure to change results from stupidity or lack of insight. Dynamic characters, on the other hand, are those who do change in a positive way. Make a list of the characters in the play and decide which ones are static and which are dynamic. What are your reasons for placing each character in the category to which you have assigned him or her? Discuss how these characters' growth or lack thereof reflects on the theme of female submission.

29 Throughout the play, many of the characters insult one another. Make a list of insults in the play and see if you can determine what cultural values those insults imply. To what extent are those values the same as or different from those of today? What factors have caused changes in the values?

30 Compare and contrast the way Petruchio treats Katherina to the way he treats his servants. Because there are differences in his treatment of her, some might argue that Petruchio does not want Katherina to be his servant but, rather, that he wants her to be his wife. Do you agree or disagree with that idea? Explain your reasons for your opinion.

31 In the scene at the end of the play when Petruchio orders Katherina to return to the banquet hall and bring Bianca and the Widow with her, when she arrives he begins by saying, "Katherina, that cap of yours becomes you not; / Off with that bable, throw it under-foot" (Act 5, Scene 2, lines 121–122). However, as Margaret Rose Jaster points out, Petruchio's order to Katherina to throw her hat on the ground is unnecessary in that she has already amply demonstrated that she will obey him. Why do you suppose Shakespeare included this piece of action?

32 Although Katherina appears to be a changed person at the end of the play, she nevertheless brings Bianca and the Widow to the banquet hall by force. What scene is this situation similar to from early in the play? How does it differ from the earlier scene? Does Katherina's behavior in this scene reinforce or undermine the notion that she is truly changed? Why do you think so?

33 At one time there was a tradition in England that required the bride, during the marriage ceremony, to kneel and kiss her husband's right foot in order to show her submission to her husband (Boose 182). However, in *The Taming of the Shrew*, instead of occurring during the marriage ceremony, Katherina offers, during her speech at the end of the play, to place her hand beneath Petruchio's foot. What do you suppose the implications of the timing of this action on Katherina's part are? Do you think Shakespeare was trying to convey anything in particular by including this offer in Katherina's speech? Why or why not?

34 Many people think that Katherina is not sincere at the end of the play when she lectures Bianca and the Widow about the wife's duty to her husband. Do you think she is sincere? Or is she being sarcastic or ironic or something else? Explain your reasons based on what happens in the play.

35 In some performances of the play, the actress playing Katherina has put her hand under Petruchio's foot and then tipped him backwards at the end of her speech about a wife's duty to her husband. In other performances, the actress playing Katherina has winked at the audience at the end of that speech. If you were a director of a play or movie version of *The Taming of the Shrew*, how would you tell the actors to perform the final scene of the play? Explain your reasons for your decisions.

36 Think of a modern movie or song that reflects conflict either between a specific male and female or between males and females in general. What are the issues involved? How are the characters dealing with those issues? Is one gender "winning" the conflict? Now compare and contrast this movie or song with *The Taming of the Shrew*.

37 People familiar with other plays by Shakespeare have noted that the females, particularly those who are the main characters, are usually more admirable than most of the males; in most cases the women are smarter, braver, and kinder than the men. Would you say that this is the case with Katherina and Petruchio? Explain your reasons for your opinion.

38 If you were to rewrite the ending of the play so that Petruchio renounces his desire to "tame" Katherina and declares instead that she is his equal in their relationship, what other changes would you need to make in the things that happen in the play for his speech to make sense? Write a speech for Petruchio to replace Katherina's speech that would indicate his changed attitude.

Sources

Barton, Ann. "*The Taming of the Shrew*: Essay." *The Riverside Shakespeare*. 2nd ed. Boston: Houghton Mifflin, 1997. 138–141.

Benson, Sean. " 'If I Do Prove Her Haggard': Shakespeare's Application of Hawking Tropes to Marriage." *Studies in Philology* 103.2 (2006). Literature Online (LION). Moraine Valley C.C. Lib., Palos Hills, IL. 25 Mar. 2008.

Boose, Lynda E. "Scolding Brides and Bridling Scolds: Taming the Woman's Unruly Member." *Shakespeare Quarterly* 42.2 (1991): 179–213.

Crocker, Holly. "Affective Resistance: Performing Passivity and Playing A-part in *The Taming of the Shrew*." *Shakespeare Quarterly* 54.2 (2003): 142–159.

Frye, Northrop. *The Myth of Deliverance: Reflections on Shakespeare's Problem Comedies*. Toronto: U of Toronto P, 1993.

Heilman, Robert B., ed. "A Note on the Sources of *The Taming of the Shrew*." *The Taming of the Shrew*. New York: Signet, 1986. 157–160.

Jaster, Margaret Rose. "Controlling Clothes, Manipulating Mates: Petruchio's Griselda." *Shakespeare Studies* 29 (2001): 93–109.

Ranald, Margaret Loftus. *Shakespeare and His Social Context*. New York: AMS Press, 1987.

Ramsey-Kurz, Helga. "Rising Above the Bait: Kate's Transformation from Bear to Falcon." *English Studies* 88.3 (2007): 262–281.

Schuler, Robert M. "Bewitching the Shrew." *Texas Studies in Literature & Language* 46.4 (2004): 387–431.

At last! Shakespeare in Language everyone can understand...

SHAKESPEARE MADE EASY Series

Scene 7

*Macbeth's castle. Enter a **sewer** directing divers servants. Then enter* **Macbeth**.

Macbeth If it were done, when 'tis done, then 'twere well
It were done quickly: if th' assassination
Could trammel up the consequence, and catch,
With his surcease, success; that but this blow
5 Might be the be-all and the end-all here,
But here, upon this bank and shoal of time,
We'd jump the life to come. But in these cases
We still have judgement here: that we but teach
Blood instructions, which being taught return
10 To plague th'inventor: this even-handed justice
Commends th'ingredience of our poisoned chalice
To our own lips. He's here in double trust:
First, as I am his kinsman and his subject,
Strong both against the deed: then, as his host,
15 Who should against his murderer shut the door,
Not bear the knife myself. Besides, this Duncan
Hath borne his faculties so meek, hath been
So clear in his great office, that his virtues
Will plead like angels, trumpet-toungèd, against
20 The deep damnation of his taking-off;
And pity, like a naked new-born babe,
Striding the blast, or Heaven's cherubin, horsed
Upon the sightless couriers of the air,
Shall blow the horrid deed in every eye,
25 That tears shall drown the wind. I have no spur
To prick the sides of my intent, but only
Vaulting ambition, which o'erleaps itself,
And falls on th'other –

Scene 7

*A room in **Macbeth's** castle. A **Butler** and several **Waiters** cross, carrying dishes of food. Then **Macbeth** enters. He is thinking about the proposed murder of **King Duncan**.*

Macbeth If we could get away with the deed after it's done, then the quicker it were done, the better. If the murder had no consequences, and his death ensured success...If, when I strike the blow, that would be the end of it – here, right here, on this side of eternity – we'd willingly chance the life to come. But usually, we get what's coming to us here on earth. We teach the art of bloodshed, then become the victims of our own lessons. This evenhanded justice makes us swallow our own poison. [Pause] Duncan is here on double trust: first, because I'm his kinsman and his subject (both good arguments against the deed); then, because I'm his host, who should protect him from his murderer–not bear the knife. Besides, this Duncan has used his power so gently, he's been so incorruptible his great office, that his virtues will plead like angels, their tongues trumpeting the damnable horror of his murder. And pity, like a naked newborn babe or Heaven's avenging angels riding the winds, will cry the deed to everyone so that tears will blind the eye. I've nothing to spur me on but high-leaping ambition, which can often bring about one's downfall.

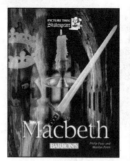
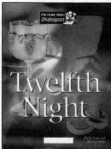

". . . as close, as word for word, as any translation of *The Canterbury Tales*."

—*The New Yorker* magazine

Chaucer's Canterbury Tales (Selected)

An Interlinear Translation, 3rd Edition

Geoffrey Chaucer,
Translated by Vincent F. Hopper,
Edited by Andrew Galloway

Meet poet Geoffrey Chaucer's immortal storytellers—the comically bawdy Miller . . . the genial and lusty Wife of Bath . . . and many others. A little more than 600 years ago, when Chaucer wrote his masterpiece, he used the English language dialect that was standard in his day. Though a rich, vital language, it's very different from the English we speak today. Vincent Hopper's critically praised translation of *The Canterbury Tales* is presented here with an enlightening introduction by pre-Renaissance literary scholar Andrew Galloway. This fine edition offers readers—

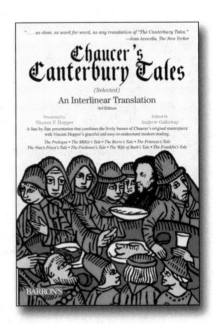

- The vigor, liveliness, and humor of Chaucer's original Middle English poetry, interspersed line-by-line with a modern, easy-to-understand translation.
- An ideal classroom text for students of English literature.

Here is an attractive and approachable version of a richly entertaining literary classic, suitable for both students and the general reader.

Paperback, ISBN 978-1-4380-0013-8
$14.99, *Canada $16.99*

Prices subject to change
without notice.

————To order————
Available at your local book store
or visit **www.barronseduc.com**

Barron's Educational Series, Inc.
250 Wireless Blvd.
Hauppauge, N.Y. 11788
Order toll-free: 1-800-645-3476
Order by fax: 1-631-434-3217

In Canada:
Georgetown Book Warehouse
34 Armstrong Ave.
Georgetown, Ontario L7G 4R9
Canadian orders: 1-800-247-7160
Order by fax: 1-800-887-1594

BARRON'S

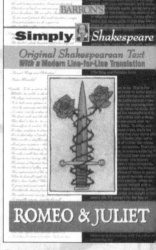

Notes